OPPOSING VIEWPOINTS® SERIES

I India

Jamuna Carroll, Book Editor

GREENHAVEN PRESS
A part of Gale, Cengage Learning

GALE
CENGAGE Learning™

Detroit • New York • San Francisco • New Haven, Conn • Waterville, Maine • London

GALE
CENGAGE Learning™

Christine Nasso, *Publisher*
Elizabeth Des Chenes, *Managing Editor*

© 2009 Greenhaven Press, a part of Gale, Cengage Learning.

Gale and Greenhaven Press are registered trademarks used herein under license.

For more information, contact:
Greenhaven Press
27500 Drake Rd.
Farmington Hills, MI 48331-3535
Or you can visit our Internet site at gale.cengage.com

For product information and technology assistance, contact us at

Gale Customer Support, 1-800-877-4253
For permission to use material from this text or product, submit all requests online at www.cengage.com/permissions

Further permissions questions can be emailed to permissionrequest@cengage.com

Articles in Greenhaven Press anthologies are often edited for length to meet page requirements. In addition, original titles of these works are changed to clearly present the main thesis and to explicitly indicate the author's opinion. Every effort is made to ensure that Greenhaven Press accurately reflects the original intent of the authors. Every effort has been made to trace the owners of copyrighted material.

Cover photograph reproduced by © 2009/Jupiterimages.

LIBRARY OF CONGRESS CATALOGING-IN-PUBLICATION DATA

India / Jamuna Carroll, book editor.
    p. cm. -- (Opposing viewpoints)
    Includes bibliographical references and index.
    ISBN 978-0-7377-4370-8 (hardcover)
    ISBN 978-0-7377-4369-2 (pbk.)
    1. India--Social conditions--21st century--Juvenile literature. 2. India--Politics and government--21st century--Juvenile literature. I. Carroll, Jamuna.
    DS407.I4456 2009
    954.05'32--dc22
                                                                    2009014561

Printed in the United States of America
1 2 3 4 5 6 7 13 12 11 10 09

Contents

Chapter 3: What Is the Status of Human Rights in India?

Chapter 4: What Efforts Would Ensure India's Future Success?

Why Consider Opposing Viewpoints?

> "The only way in which a human being can make some approach to knowing the whole of a subject is by hearing what can be said about it by persons of every variety of opinion and studying all modes in which it can be looked at by every character of mind. No wise man ever acquired his wisdom in any mode but this."
>
> John Stuart Mill

In our media-intensive culture it is not difficult to find differing opinions. Thousands of newspapers and magazines and dozens of radio and television talk shows resound with differing points of view. The difficulty lies in deciding which opinion to agree with and which "experts" seem the most credible. The more inundated we become with differing opinions and claims, the more essential it is to hone critical reading and thinking skills to evaluate these ideas. Opposing Viewpoints books address this problem directly by presenting stimulating debates that can be used to enhance and teach these skills. The varied opinions contained in each book examine many different aspects of a single issue. While examining these conveniently edited opposing views, readers can develop critical thinking skills such as the ability to compare and contrast authors' credibility, facts, argumentation styles, use of persuasive techniques, and other stylistic tools. In short, the Opposing Viewpoints Series is an ideal way to attain the higher-level thinking and reading skills so essential in a culture of diverse and contradictory opinions.

In addition to providing a tool for critical thinking, Opposing Viewpoints books challenge readers to question their own strongly held opinions and assumptions. Most people form their opinions on the basis of upbringing, peer pressure, and personal, cultural, or professional bias. By reading carefully balanced opposing views, readers must directly confront new ideas as well as the opinions of those with whom they disagree. This is not to simplistically argue that everyone who reads opposing views will—or should—change his or her opinion. Instead, the series enhances readers' understanding of their own views by encouraging confrontation with opposing ideas. Careful examination of others' views can lead to the readers' understanding of the logical inconsistencies in their own opinions, perspective on why they hold an opinion, and the consideration of the possibility that their opinion requires further evaluation.

Evaluating Other Opinions

To ensure that this type of examination occurs, Opposing Viewpoints books present all types of opinions. Prominent spokespeople on different sides of each issue as well as well-known professionals from many disciplines challenge the reader. An additional goal of the series is to provide a forum for other, less known, or even unpopular viewpoints. The opinion of an ordinary person who has had to make the decision to cut off life support from a terminally ill relative, for example, may be just as valuable and provide just as much insight as a medical ethicist's professional opinion. The editors have two additional purposes in including these less known views. One, the editors encourage readers to respect others' opinions—even when not enhanced by professional credibility. It is only by reading or listening to and objectively evaluating others' ideas that one can determine whether they are worthy of consideration. Two, the inclusion of such viewpoints encourages the important critical thinking skill of objectively evaluating an author's credentials and bias. This evaluation will illuminate an author's reasons for taking a particular stance on an issue and will aid in readers' evaluation of the author's ideas.

It is our hope that these books will give readers a deeper understanding of the issues debated and an appreciation of the complexity of even seemingly simple issues when good and honest people disagree. This awareness is particularly important in a democratic society such as ours in which people enter into public debate to determine the common good. Those with whom one disagrees should not be regarded as enemies but rather as people whose views deserve careful examination and may shed light on one's own.

Thomas Jefferson once said that "difference of opinion leads to inquiry, and inquiry to truth." Jefferson, a broadly educated man, argued that "if a nation expects to be ignorant and free . . . it expects what never was and never will be." As individuals and as a nation, it is imperative that we consider the opinions of others and examine them with skill and discernment. The Opposing Viewpoints Series is intended to help readers achieve this goal.

David L. Bender and Bruno Leone,
Founders

Introduction

> *"The central question in any discussion of pluralism in contemporary India is how a vast, multi-ethnic country—in terms of religion, language, community, caste and tribe—has survived as a democratic state and society in conditions not very conducive to the sustenance of democracy—underdevelopment, mass poverty, illiteracy and extreme regional disparities."*
>
> *—Professor Zoya Hasan,*
> *Jawaharlal Nehru University*

With a staggering 1.15 billion inhabitants, India is the world's largest democracy. Remarkably, India has maintained democracy while also being one of the most plural societies in the world. Across its twenty-eight states and seven union territories, the subcontinent displays what blogger Mohit Joshi sums up as "mind-boggling diversity. Travel just 100 miles and you are in a different world—language changes, food changes, level of development changes, attires and lifestyles change."

Home to people of nearly every world religion, India is populated by over 800 million Hindus, nearly 150 million Muslims, 24 million Christians, and many others. It is the birthplace of multiple religions, including Hinduism, Buddhism, Sikhism, and Jainism. The country has about twenty national languages and hundreds of mother languages. The denomination on Indian rupee banknotes is printed in fifteen languages, and street signs in some places are posted in four. Indian customs, clothing, and celebrations also vary from state to state and village to village.

To safeguard the rights and interests of its plural population, India was founded as a secular, democratic republic with a multiparty political system. In the words of Indian politician M. Veerappa Moily, "Secularism suits the genius of a multi-religious, multi-caste and multi-lingual country like India best. The secular ethos, furrowed deep by Mahatma Gandhi in the minds of India, nurtured a sense of tolerance that had kept society together as well as democratic." Yet this has not been without a struggle.

India's diverse communities sometimes clash, threatening India's unity. Hindus and Muslims have fought on and off since Muslims invaded the country in 715. By 1947, when Britain prepared to grant India its independence, bitterness between the Hindu majority and the Muslim minority was unignorable. Some Hindus harbored resentment against Muslims tracing back to the invasion. A number of Muslims felt they would not be fairly represented in a country dominated by Hindus, whose religion, lifestyle, and laws were unlike their own. They pushed for a partition of India. Borders were drawn at the northeast and northwest corners of the country, where a majority of Muslims lived. These became East Pakistan and West Pakistan, together forming the Islamic Republic of Pakistan. The divisions displaced 16 million people who scrambled to cross the border into or out of India. One million perished in the fighting. Exacerbating matters, the two countries immediately went to war over the region of Kashmir, a dispute which continues to this day.

All these incidents served to deepen tensions between Hindus and Muslims still living in India. Violent skirmishes ensued, and still occur today. One of the bloodiest occurred in Gujarat in 2002, when religious riots broke out between Muslims and Hindus. Frenzied mobs descended on villages, beating and torturing people, raping women, and burning families to death. Nearly two thousand people were killed, the majority of them Muslim. Besides being an atrocious reminder of deep-seated ill will between the peoples, the incident raised the question of state-sponsored prejudice against Muslims. Some authorities allegedly ignored Muslims' pleas for help during the incident, and afterward the government awarded Hindu families twice as much in compensation for each person killed as Muslim families were offered.

Some have protested the treatment of Muslims by turning to terrorism. In November 2008, ten young members of a Pakistani terrorist organization coordinated bombings at hotels, a hospital, a rail station, and other busy locations in Mumbai, the capital city of Maharashtra. Armed with guns and grenades, they took hostages and a siege continued for days. More than 160 innocent people were killed and over three hundred injured. A message sent to Indian media outlets claimed responsibility for the attacks: "We want to warn the Indian government that they must stop the injustice against the Muslim community."

Preserving the interests of Hindus, Muslims, and the rest of the population in a democratic setting is an arduous task. In "The Unbearable Lightness of Diversity," Mohit Joshi highlights the difficulties: "The private and public cost of catering to myriad groups of people is staggering, the schisms created by radically diverse interests are deep, the task of development is ridden with partisan ideologies."

Internal affairs professor George C. Thomas suggests that democracy itself can be divisive. "Democracy has the ability to empower minorities and promote equality," he posits, "but it can just as easily exacerbate divisions. When voting tends to take place along ethnic lines, majority rule can result in the subjugation of the minority voice. Not only does this foster an unequal society, it also has the potential to destabilize the entire state." The losing minority may, for example, throw out the democratic process and attempt to secede from the nation.

It is against the odds that India has succeeded in sustaining both democracy and diversity. But will democracy survive over the long term? And can peace prevail between religious and ethnic groups as variant as India's? *Opposing Viewpoints: India* is a compendium of views on such questions. Analysts, politicians, and commentators from India and abroad discuss contentious topics in the following chapters: "What Is India's Global Impact?" "What Are India's Most Serious Crises?" "What Is the Status of Human Rights in India?" and "What Efforts Would Ensure India's Future Success?" With hope, as India grows into a global giant, it will retain its status as the most culturally, religiously, and linguistically diverse democracy in the world.

CHAPTER 1

What Is India's Global Impact?

Chapter Preface

When India was partitioned in 1947, creating the nation of Pakistan, it happened amidst bitterness and chaos. The two countries immediately declared war, the first of three to be fought between them. Then the longstanding feud threatened to turn nuclear. International attention was drawn at critical points in May 1998, when India and Pakistan both conducted nuclear bomb tests, and again in 1999 and early 2002. Though the situations were defused, some believe that India, with an estimated one hundred warheads, still poses a danger to Pakistan, South Asia, and the world.

The most recent nuclear crisis between India and its neighbor occurred after a deadly attack on India's Parliament in December 2001. Five Pakistanis from a terrorist organization killed seven people that day. India claimed that their terrorist group was supported by Pakistan. When India made demands and its neighbor refused, both countries mobilized their troops. A million soldiers lined up on both sides of the border prepared to fight. Nuclear capable missiles were deployed. Words between the countries' leaders grew fierce. India's Defence Secretary Yogendra Narain made a chilling statement in a June 2002 interview: "A surgical strike is the answer." If that does not work, he cautioned, "We must be prepared for total mutual destruction." Adding to the furor, Pakistan conducted three missile tests. Gaurav Kampani, senior research associate at the Center for Nonproliferation Studies, describes tensions at the time: "Indian and Pakistani political and military leaders openly engaged in nuclear saber rattling and traded threats. The readiness and alert levels of nuclear forces and their associated delivery systems were raised, all of which added to concerns about crisis stability in the region."

Some experts thought nuclear war was eminent, while others were less certain. All recognized the fragility of the situation because the two countries share a border. If missiles were launched by one side, they could land on the other in less than ten minutes. This also means each country would have a very short time to make crisis decisions. The U.S. Pentagon produced a report with frightening death toll estimations. A nuclear event between Pakistan and India, it said, would likely kill 12 million, with millions more injured and exposed to radiation. Furthermore, experts projected that a nuclear bomb and the fires it would spark would affect temperatures and precipitation across the globe for years. Crops would be decimated and one billion people would die from starvation alone.

So, it was to the world's great relief when the 2002 nuclear standoff de-escalated. South Asia expert Steve Coll describes it this way:

> India concluded, correctly, that as frustrating as it was, they could not accomplish anything in war that would be worth the price of waging that war. India's economy was racing ahead. India was breaking out into a new century of great-power status and prosperity, and the infrastructure of terror in Pakistan unfortunately cannot be destroyed by military means alone.

The troops began to disassemble and the nations signed a cease-fire. Peace talks began in 2004.

The ways in which India interacts with other countries and whether it does so wisely is debated in the following chapter. Though in this example India could make a negative impact of global magnitude, it is hoped that through peaceful dealings with Pakistan and other countries, India's global influence will ultimately be a positive one.

| "An Energy Revolution is needed in India."

India Must Cap Its CO_2 Emissions to Help Prevent Global Warming

G. Ananthapadmanabhan, K. Srinivas, and Vinuta Gopal

The following viewpoint is excerpted from a study conducted by G. Ananthapadmanabhan, K. Srinivas, and Vinuta Gopal on behalf of the Greenpeace India Society. The authors implore India to use less energy from fossil fuels, thereby emitting less carbon dioxide (CO_2), to curb what they call destructive global warming. While the authors concede that the majority of the country's inhabitants use little energy, they charge that India's upper and middle classes consume a disproportionately large amount. That India's overall per person CO_2 emissions are lower than the world average is no excuse for India to continue to pollute at current levels, the authors avow.

As you read, consider the following questions:

1. What do the authors predict will happen if the upper and middle classes do not reduce their emissions?

2. Name three effects of increased global temperatures, as stated by the authors.

3. According to the authors, what is India's average per capita emission of carbon dioxide?

Climate change is today accepted as the largest threat to humanity and is now taking centre stage globally with discussions in various international governmental, economic and academic fora. It has brought to focus attention on the critical question of linkages between development and environmental sustainability.

In December 2007, the world's governments will meet in Bali, Indonesia to kick-start the process leading up to the second commitment period of the Kyoto Protocol. This meeting is extremely crucial to ensure that governments commit to larger emission cuts that will keep global temperature rise to below 2 degrees. While this international meeting sets the debate for 'climate justice' at a global level this study aims at raising the same debate within the country. It asks the question—Is there climate injustice happening in India? It presents a case for the Indian government to implement the principle of 'common but differentiated responsibilities' amongst the various socioeconomic groups in the country.

The report is based on a first of its kind face-to-face survey across the country ranging from the metros to medium and small towns and rural areas on domestic energy consumption and transportation. The energy consumption patterns in 819 households have been converted into CO_2 [carbon dioxide] emissions and then assigned to seven different income classes.

The findings plainly illustrate that the considerably significant carbon footprint of a relatively small wealthy class (1% of the population) in the country is camouflaged by the 823 million poor population of the country, who keep the overall per capita emissions below 2 tonnes of CO_2 per year. While even the richest income class in this study, earning more than 30,000 rupees a month, produce slightly less than the global average CO_2 emissions of 5 tonnes, this amount already exceeds a sustainable global average CO_2 emissions of 2.5 tonnes per capita that needs to be reached to limit global warming below 2 degrees centigrade. The carbon footprint of the 4 highest income classes earning more than 8,000 rupees per month, representing a population of about 150 million people in the country, already exceeds sustainable levels. . . .

The average per capita emissions of the different socioeconomic groups in India are quite literally worlds apart.

Two Indias

While India has a right to demand a 'common but differentiated' responsibility at an international level, there is the urgent need for intra-national common but differentiated responsibility too. Developed nations need to cut their CO_2 emissions not only to prevent climate change but also to give space to the developing world to catch up, without pushing the global temperatures over the tipping point. The same is true within India. If the upper and the middle class do not manage to check their CO_2 emissions, they will not only contribute to global warming, but will also deny hundreds of millions of poor Indians access to development. The study clearly illustrates the growing schism of carbon emissions between the two Indias; the poor bearing the biggest climate impact burden and camouflaging the other India's lifestyle choices.

The prescription provided as a response to the results in the study is not that India should not develop or the wealthy should stop consuming, but to make a clear case for India to decarbonise its development. The path of 11th and 12th Five Year Plans proposed by the Indian government continues to base the future of energy production in the country mainly on coal power plants, thus further increasing CO_2 emissions. A major revision of the future of the power sector is needed, shifting investments from coal and nuclear to renewables and energy efficiency, to create the carbon space for the poor to develop. In short, an Energy Revolution is needed in India as well as the rest of the world.

Globally, temperatures have already increased by 0.7 degrees centigrade over the past century. Temperatures are expected to further increase by a minimum of 1.8 degrees centigrade to a maximum of 4 degrees centigrade until the end of this century depending on our ability (or inability) to check climate change by undertaking drastic reductions in emissions of Greenhouse Gases (GHGs). Apart from a few positive impacts on tourism and agriculture in Northern Europe, increase in global temperatures will have detrimental effects in most parts of the world. Changing rainfall patterns will result in intense flooding and severe droughts, melting glaciers will aggravate the problem of fresh water shortage. The intensity and frequency of cyclones and other storms will increase, vector borne diseases will spread and rising sea-levels will eventually drown coastal low lying mega cities like Mumbai and Kolkata. Developing economies located in tropical regions will have to bear the brunt of the worst impacts of climate change; countries like India which are on a high growth path will find their development jeopardized if global temperatures rise above 2 degrees centigrade.

Climate change is man-made. The globe is heating up due to the emission of GHGs, the most prominent being carbon dioxide produced by burning fossil fuels. Historically, developed countries are the biggest contributors to excessive GHG emissions, making them the most responsible for climate change. However, over the last few decades, emissions of rapidly developing economies like India have surged. In fact, rankings by the WRI [World Research Institute] of top GHG emitters has USA on top, and developing countries such as China and India are ranked at No 2 and No 5 respectively, making them amongst the world's biggest emitters.

India Must Reduce Its Emissions

India's overall average per capita CO_2 emission is 1.67 tonnes. The figure has been arrived at dividing the overall CO_2 emissions of India given by the World Research Institute, by the population size given by the CIA Factbook. The average annual per capita CO_2 emission in India as assessed by this survey is 501 kg. This is 33% of the overall Indian per capita emissions, which is in line with the secotral division of CO_2 assessed by WRI. Besides the assessed emissions generated from energy consumption in transport and household, the personal carbon foot print also includes CO_2 emissions generated from food and non food consumption and additional overheads due to public consumption.

The average CO_2 emissions per income group range from 335 kg for the income class below 3,000 rupees per month to an average of 1,494 kg for the income classes above 30,000 rupees per month. The richest consumer classes produce 4.5 times more CO_2 than the poorest class, and almost 3 times more than the average Indian (501 kgs)....

Per Capita Annual CO_2 Emissions by Income Group

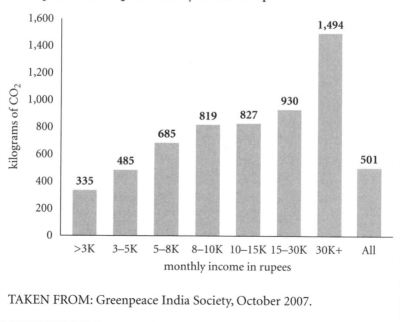

TAKEN FROM: Greenpeace India Society, October 2007.

The next round of negotiations for the second phase of the Kyoto Protocol, covering the period after 2012 should start this December [2007] in Bali. Governments are busy debating about who to blame and who must commit to drastic emission cuts to save the world from climate change. Until now, the Indian government has maintained that the average per capita CO_2 emission of India is low (below 2 tonnes per person) compared to that of EU-25 states (10.5 tonnes) and the US (23 tonnes). This is the basis for their argument to continue on a fossil fuel driven economic development pathway.

Referring to the principle of common but differentiated responsibilities, India claims its right to development and thus its right to consume more energy from fossil fuels, asking developed nations to create the carbon space. Implicit in this is the notion that the developed countries need to decrease their CO_2 emissions drastically, so that developing countries can still increase theirs without pushing the planet in the direction of climate chaos.

But India at this point of time is faced by two sharply contradictory realities. On the one hand there is a rapidly growing rich consumer class which has made the country the 12th largest luxury market in the world; on the other hand India is home to more than 800 million poor people on the planet who are extremely vulnerable to the impacts of climate change. . . .

Though all the Indian income classes stay below the world average per capita CO_2 emission, unfortunately such a view misses out the third dimension of climate justice. Namely that the global distribution of CO_2 emissions needs not only to be equitable, but also sustainable. Today's CO_2 emissions already lead to a steady increase of global temperature, and with a global population still rising, an average CO_2 emission of 5 tonnes would drive the planet into a state of climate crisis.

To achieve the needed reduction of global CO_2 emissions to check climate change, average world CO_2 emissions needs to be brought down to 2.5 tonnes per capita by 2030. In India 150 million people who today earn more than 8,000 rupees per month already emit more than 2.5 tonnes CO_2 per annum (sustainable global average per capita CO_2 emission). To create the space for the remaining 980 million people in the country to develop without heating the planet above 2 degree centigrade, India needs to find ways to reduce the CO_2 emissions of the upper 150 million people.

> *"India has long resisted signing up to any mandatory cuts, saying the impact on its growing economy will be too severe."*

India Should Not Be Required to Reduce CO$_2$ Emissions

Iain Murray

In this viewpoint, Iain Murray discusses India's energy policy and finds that the country needs and wants to become more energy efficient, but the reason is not to cut carbon emissions. Instead, India hopes to use its resources effectively and continue to grow the economy so that billions of Indians can rise out of poverty. Murray is a senior fellow at the Competitive Enterprise Institute and regularly contributes to National Review *and* National Review Online.

As you read, consider the following questions:

1. What is a disadvantage of biofuels when compared with nuclear and coal power?

2. What is India's emerging energy policy focused on?

Iain Murray, "India Adapts," *National Review Online*, July 18, 2007. Reproduced by permission of the author.

3. What environmental and resource model is favored by the Europeans and how is it different from the Indian model?

Deepak Lal has a typically thoughtful essay in New Delhi's *Business-Standard*. He finds there are many reasons for India to rethink its energy policy, but that global warming is not one of them:

> By contrast, the estimates I made for the Planning Commission in the early 1970s (see Lal: *Prices for Planning*, HEB, 1980) based on the same methodology as the *Stern Review*, but with more plausible parameters, yielded a social discount rate of 7 percent for India. At this discount rate, the present value of Re 1 accruing 75 years from today would be worth nothing, making most of the speculative economic costs and benefits, and the apocalyptic predictions of the *Stern Review*, irrelevant for India.

> This does not downgrade the serious current environmental problems caused by rapid growth in India and China. Anyone who has choked in the fetid air of Chungking, Xian, Beijing or Delhi will know that no climate scares are needed to provide a case for dealing with their unhealthy air pollution. Similarly India and China face a growing water crisis irrespective of what is happening to global CO_2 emissions. Subsidies to energy and water use need to be removed for efficiency reasons. Whilst, given the political instability and growing political determination of supplies of fossil fuels from the countries where they are concentrated, it is sensible to diversify energy sources. Both nuclear power and India's coal reserves provide more secure alternatives. Bio fuels, by contrast, have the disadvantage of competing for limited land with essentials like food. However, the sun, which most probably controls the climate, also offers the backstop technology which will provide the unbounded energy for India's continuing economic growth. In thinking about all these economic issues, the changing climate is a red herring.

A UCLA Professor Argues That India Must Be Permitted to Burn Fossil Fuels

The Industrial Revolution, which launched the era of modern intensive growth, was based on the transformation of an organic agrarian economy whose growth was ultimately bounded by a fixed factor, land, to a mineral-energy-using economy where the supply of energy from fossil fuels was for all practical purposes unbounded. This removed the constraints to a sustained rise in per capita income. Mass structural poverty need no longer be the inevitable fate of humankind. This process of transforming an organic into a mineral-energy-using economy, which India has fitfully engaged in, has already lifted millions out of poverty. For a full elimination of this ancient scourge India will have to consume even more energy from fossil fuels, which we are told will lead to global warming. I remain deeply skeptical (as do many others) about the underlying science and the dire effects predicted about global warming. But if India is forced to limit its green-house emissions front burning fossil fuels, it will indubitably condemn millions of poor Indians to perpetual poverty.

The attempt by environmental nongovernmental organizations like Greenpeace to push their agenda on a host of issues ... also threatens the livelihood and welfare of millions of Indians. India needs to beat off these threats to its poor....

Deepak Lal,
Population and Development Review, *supp., 2006.*

An Emerging Energy Policy

It appears the Indian government is following Prof. Lal's advice, while still giving lip service to "climate change." Its emerging policy is focused on adaptation, not emissions targets:

> The growing needs of the Indian economy put pressure on national resources, he said.
>
> The council will work on a strategy to offset the impact of melting Himalayan glaciers which feed many of the country's rivers and are a major source of water and power.
>
> A tree planting programme will also be launched to replenish 15m acres of degraded forests.
>
> And the council will come up with a road map for energy-efficient approaches to economic development.
>
> But no mention was made of cutting carbon emissions.
>
> India has long resisted signing up to any mandatory cuts, saying the impact on its growing economy will be too severe.

As the developing world seeks to square long-run environmental and resource concerns with the immediate necessity of lifting billions rapidly out of poverty, the Indian model is likely to be much more attractive than the carbon-constrained model favored by European technocrats.

*"The net effect of outsourcing on the
U.S. economy is likely positive."*

Outsourcing Jobs Benefits
India and the United States

Daniel W. Drezner

*Daniel W. Drezner is professor of international politics at Tufts
University and senior editor at the* National Interest. *In the
viewpoint that follows, he alleges that the media and politicians
exaggerate the negative effects of outsourcing jobs to India while
ignoring the benefits. In his opinion, downturns in the job market can be attributed to causes other than outsourcing. In fact,
outsourcing jobs in one sector, he contends, creates job positions
in others. Furthermore, he asserts, offshoring to India increases
demand for American products there and ultimately boosts the
U.S. economy. Besides, Drezner claims, few Americans lose their
jobs to outsourcing.*

As you read, consider the following questions:

1. What percentage of mass layoffs in the United States is
   due to outsourcing, according to statistics cited by the
   author?

2. In Drezner's contention, what sectors have new jobs as a result of outsourcing?

3. What three policy recommendations does the author make to calm American workers' fears over offshoring?

The best way to understand the growth of offshoring and outsourcing is to realize that "it's the technology, stupid." What's happened in the last 10 years or so is that the reduction of communication costs and standardization of software packages has fundamentally altered the way some jobs are done. Some tasks that were previously considered very complex—from office work to data analysis—have been simplified with the standardization of software packages. In addition, the growth of the Internet has made it possible to have people do tasks overseas—from anywhere. Nandan Nilekani, the chief executive of Infosys Technologies, an India-based IT firm, has said that "everything you can send down a wire is up for grabs," and while that may be a bit of an exaggeration, it's become at least potentially feasible to have people perform certain tasks almost anywhere, tasks that were not portable before.

This change has affected even the most hallowed of professions—journalism. In February 2004, Reuters announced it would outsource six low-level financial reporting jobs to journalists in India. Coincidentally, the number of newspaper stories that mentioned "offshoring" doubled between January and February of last year. By the end of that month, the outsourcing phenomenon was the cover story of *The Economist, Time, Business Week*, and *Wired*. There's an old saying: when a neighbor loses their job, it's a downturn; when you lose your job, it's a recession; when journalists lose theirs, it's a depression.

There's no question that the effects of outsourcing and offshoring on the U.S. economy and job picture have been exaggerated. Since 2004 was an election year, outsourcing made a convenient scapegoat for politicians. It's very easy to call attention to the direct costs of a job being created in India. The benefits, on the other hand, are there, and just as real, but they are much more indirect. Also, the fact that as of 2003–2004, the job market in the United States still looked sluggish led many to think that jobs must be going elsewhere.

But these really are correspondences, not connections. According to the Bureau of Labor Statistics, less than 3 percent of mass layoffs by U.S. firms can be traced to offshore outsourcing. This is of little comfort to American workers, however: unemployment, as an issue, is a lot like crime, in the sense that people perceive that a much larger fraction of the population is affected than is actually the case. It isn't so much what the raw numbers show, but whether you know someone—or know someone who knows someone who knows someone—who's lost a job to outsourcing.

Another issue that intersects with offshoring is that over the past few years the distribution of gains in the economy has been going more to owners of capital than has historically been the case. One possible explanation is that offshoring has weakened the bargaining power of workers vis-à-vis CEOs, allowing management to appropriate the productivity gains reaped from offshoring. The problem with that explanation is that it can be difficult to distinguish what's being caused by offshoring and what's being caused by broader economic transformations, such as technological change. For example, the Bureau of Labor Statistics estimated that fewer than 5,000 workers were laid off en masse due to offshoring in the first quarter of 2004; in January of last year, Kodak announced a mass layoff of 15,000 workers—because the growth of digital photography reduced demand for film. This year Kodak announced additional layoffs of 10,000 workers. Furthermore, a lot of the jobs that are sent overseas are jobs that might not continue to exist in the United States in any case: If those jobs are not outsourced overseas, they might be automated or otherwise eliminated through technological innovation.

Overall, the net effect of outsourcing on the U.S. economy is likely positive. What makes this assertion difficult to prove is that the jobs created as a result of this phenomenon are not necessarily going to be in the areas in which we've been outsourcing—data services, software, etc. It's more likely that they'll be in construction, retail, or other sectors that cater to the domestic economy. A growing U.S. economy means firms will be reinvesting their gains here, expanding and thus creating increased demand for economic goods and services across the board.

When economist N. Gregory Mankiw, the former chairman of the Council of Economic Advisors, said that outsourcing was simply another form of trade, he got beaten up politically. He was still 100 percent correct. As an economic phenomenon, the outsourcing of services is really no different than trade in manufactured goods. What's politically different is that the people who are affected are those who had seen themselves as economic winners—people who'd never thought of themselves as competing in a global marketplace. Manufacturing workers in particular probably have quite a sense of "schadenfreude" about the whole outsourcing phenomenon, watching service workers suddenly coming to the realization, "This is how the free market works?"

Capital Abroad

From the U.S. perspective, India is often seen as the big winner from outsourcing. What's interesting is that there are political tensions developing within India that echo what we're experiencing in the United States. Both countries are experiencing overall economic gains, but an unequal distribution of benefits. In both cases there's new wealth being created that wasn't there before. India's middle class is growing at a rate that in terms of absolute numbers looks impressive from an American perspective, but as a fraction of India's population looks a little less so.

It's certainly not the case that everyone's gotten rich there; the Indian countryside remains terribly poor. Per capita income in India is well below the global median. In 2004, the BJP (Bharatiya Janata Party)—then India's ruling party— called a general election under the assumption that the 8 percent growth rate would lead inevitably to their reelection. Instead, they were thrown out of office. What the BJP hadn't counted on were the 700 million Indians reliant on the agricultural sector, who hadn't benefited at all. If there had never been outsourcing, it isn't the case that those 700 million people would have been better off—if anything, they would have been worse off. With offshore outsourcing, you have winners and losers in India; before offshore outsourcing, you only had losers.

Ironically, India itself now has some other pressing concerns because of the expansion of the global market for outsourcing services. Wage rates in Bangalore are starting to rise dramatically, and India has bottlenecks in its educational infrastructure that will limit the growth of the labor force. So other countries—the Philippines, Indonesia, Ghana—are beginning to compete. Nowadays you can even find Europeans and Americans working—if only temporarily—in India. Backpackers hiking through India stop off in Bangalore and work in call centers for a few weeks to pay their way.

What you're likely to start seeing is a hierarchy of services, with India not holding on to the really basic jobs. India does have a solid leg to stand on in terms of medium-value services. But where things really are likely to take off within India is in terms of increased demand for local goods and services—a situation is developing in which the Indian economy isn't paying attention just to what the U.S. market wants, but to what the Indian market wants. And that's what's driving

Benefits of Outsourcing for the U.S. and the U.K.

- Research shows that some of the new economic activity generated in developing countries by outsourcing will generate new demand for goods and services in the country where the jobs have moved from (eg America). McKinsey Global Institute estimates that for every dollar US corporations spend on outsourcing to India, the US economy benefits by $1.14. This is based on several assumptions: that 69% of displaced service workers will find new jobs within a year, and will end up earning 96% of their previous wages—backed up by 1979–1999 data. However older workers may be out of work far longer, especially if their education is poor.

- Outsourcing saves money for corporations which means lower costs for consumers, and higher dividends for pensioners who own 75% of US and UK wealth—that means more money to spend on other things such as local services (meals out, beauty treatments, gardening, decorating etc) and that produces new jobs.

- Outsourcing has meant for example that you can buy a DVD player for less than $100. It is one reason why retail costs of products has halved in many sectors over the last 20 years, allowing for inflation.

Patrick Dixon,
"The Future of Outsourcing,"
GlobalChange.com.

these associated booms in construction and retail. The benefits that were initially concentrated in the IT [information technology] industry are now diffusing through the rest of the Indian economy.

Technology and trade have always destroyed jobs in the United States—what Joseph Schumpeter called "creative destruction," because along the way these twin forces created even more jobs. What is likely to happen in the future is that some U.S. jobs will continue to move overseas, but on the other hand, as other economies—like India's—continue to grow much richer, they are going to start demanding an increasing number of U.S. products. If you examine the trade data on services classically thought of as part of IT and business services offshoring, you'll see that the United States is running a trade surplus in most of those areas. Even the trend is encouraging. Between 1997 and 2002, annual imports of business, technical, and professional services increased by $16.3 billion—but during that same half decade, exports of those services increased by $20.5 billion. This is not surprising, since the higher-value-added services still tend to stay in the United States.

A lot of U.S. firms that looked into offshoring have now tried it, found there were a lot of hidden costs associated with it, and retrenched and moved operations closer to home; the process is known as "homeshoring" or "nearshoring." For example, there are Silicon Valley firms that experimented with offshore call centers in Bangalore, found them too costly, and decided to outsource operations to Oklahoma instead.

The reason the United States has benefited from globalization is that labor markets here are so flexible. The McKinsey Global Institute has compared the effect of offshoring in the United States and key EU [European Union] countries. They found that offshoring was a net gain for the United States, because labor markets were flexible enough for displaced workers to find new jobs. For the EU countries, labor markets are so rigid that they are net losers from offshoring.

On the policy side, the U.S. government should do everything it can to maintain that flexibility without increasing economic insecurity unreasonably. And a key measure would be to ensure portability of health care coverage, because workers are quite understandably scared about the possibility of losing their benefits if they lose their jobs. If you can create a scenario where health care is portable rather than tied to employers that would reduce a lot of the anxiety over potential job losses due to outsourcing. Similarly, things like education and retraining programs are worthy of greater investments—but that's true regardless of the outsourcing phenomenon.

The political future will depend fundamentally on the overall state of employment. The numbers imply that there was actually more outsourcing during the 1990s than there is now, but no one cared since overall job creation figures were so robust that nobody really lost out. If the job picture remains weak, outsourcing will continue to be a political hot button.

Economics is not a zero-sum game. The fact that a middle class is developing in India does not automatically mean the middle class in the United States is threatened. The nice thing about economics is that it's a win-win game. As outsourcing makes Indians richer, the process should actually translate into Americans profiting—not only from Indian demand for American products but also from improved economic efficiency and greater economic growth in the United States.

| *"Money earned from offshoring cannot significantly raise the living conditions of the average Indian."*

Outsourcing Jobs Has Negative Long-Term Effects on India

Rabindra P. Kar

In the following viewpoint, Rabindra P. Kar blasts assumptions that the offshoring of jobs from Western countries is beneficial for India. Though he concedes that offshoring may hold short-term benefits for India, Kar sees the long-term picture as bleak. India spends too much time attracting foreign jobs and too little developing its own technologies and solutions to problems at home, he claims. Worse, he warns, Western corporations require workers to enter intellectual property agreements that make Indians hand over rights to their discoveries. Kar, a software developer, is an activist on work-visa and outsourcing issues.

As you read, consider the following questions:

1. How has the sudden influx of jobs affected urban India areas, in the author's assertion?

2. According to Kar, what developments in biotechnology and pharmaceuticals are needed in India?

3. What types of intellectual property does Kar say become the property of Western corporations when they contract with Indian BPO (Business Process Outsourcing) firms?

In recent years, there has been a vigorous, sometimes acrimonious, debate about whether offshoring (also referred to as "outsourcing") is positive or negative for the United States and the other developed Western economies. Underlying this debate is an unspoken assumption—that offshoring has been very good for the developing countries where the jobs have moved. India is widely regarded as the prime beneficiary of this phenomenon. Consequently, it seems like a rhetorical question to ask whether offshoring is good for India.

If we consider the recent past, since the early 1990s, the general consensus is that offshoring has been a big positive for India. It has been a big factor in changing India's image from a land of poverty and social "backwardness" into a potential economic superpower. It has spawned an information technology industry with exports of more than US$10 billion annually. It has greatly slowed, if not reversed, the "brain-drain" of educated and talented Indians to the West.

An Unsustainable Strategy

Of course, there have been negatives too. The sudden influx of companies and jobs into a few urban areas, notably Bangalore and New Delhi's suburbs, has overwhelmed the existing poor infrastructure, leading to impossibly congested roads as well as water and electricity shortages. The huge inflation in land and housing prices in urban areas has hit the common man hard because the average Indian's income is puny compared to what the *nouveau-riche* techies earn. On balance though, the offshoring wave has benefited India, both psychologically and economically. At least so far.

Can India ride this wave to economic stardom in the next generation? Long-term, is offshoring good for India?

The central premise of this [viewpoint] is that while offshoring has been good for India in the short-term, the long-term negatives will outweigh the positives. Since that is both a counter-intuitive and controversial assertion, the rest of this [viewpoint] will deal with the pitfalls of offshoring as a driver of India's socioeconomic destiny.

Let's start by looking at offshoring's employment potential. Estimates in the US media of the number of jobs currently outsourced to India range between 400,000 and 700,000. The most highly publicized outsourcing estimate, by Forrester Research (2004), predicted that 3.3 million US jobs would be offshored by 2015. Even if (a big if) India got a big majority of them, that amounts to at most 2.5 million jobs. If in the same period the European Union, Japan, Australia and Canada combined outsourced twice as many jobs as the US, that would total 7.5 million jobs in 2015.

Now consider that India's population in 2015 will be nearly 1.2 billion people, which implies an adult workforce of 300 million or more. Thus even the optimistic predictions are that no more than 2.5% of India's workforce will be employed in offshore services. Yet today, both India's central government and many "progressive" state governments are obsessively focused on attracting offshore work—spending precious resources to create technology zones, offering tax incentives and lavishing time and attention on pitches to multinational corporate executives. If India's population were similar to South Korea or Taiwan (in the tens of millions), providing offshore services could have been a big part of its future employment plans. But a nation containing one-sixth of humanity cannot achieve prosperity by taking jobs from other nations with much smaller populations. That is simply not a long-term, sustainable strategy.

Outsourced Jobs Do Not Teach Indians Valuable Job Skills

If a call center operator learns how to manage a client in America, can his skills be transferred readily to other areas? If the outsourcing sector slows down, can he join an Indian-based call center, considering that there are not many call center services in India?. . .

The point is that the majority of the skills learned in this sector cannot add value to a job required to service India. That is a major problem.

Suhit Anantula,
"Is Outsourcing Good for India?" OhmyNews International,
May 24, 2006. http://english.ohmynews.com.

Unrealistic Expectations and Limited Resources

A more subtle problem with the offshoring boom, is that it is giving urban Indians unrealistic expectations and distorted goals. The middle-class in India and China now believe that as the jobs move to Asia, they will be able to enjoy the consumption-heavy living standards of middle-class Westerners—two cars, a big, single-family, centrally air-conditioned home; all the electronic gizmos that their hearts desire, and so on. Their dreams of gizmos galore are achievable, since electronic goods keep getting cheaper and more plentiful. But there are some huge obstacles in the way of the other expectations—namely population size, population density, energy constraints and environmental limits.

First consider the effects of widespread automobile ownership. If just one-third of China and India's combined population could afford the US norm of one car per adult, that would be 800 million more cars in these two countries alone.

With the world now struggling with oil at more than US$60 per barrel, what would the price of oil be then? If the 200 million cars in the US produce such damaging levels of pollution and global-warming, can our planet withstand a three- or four-fold increase in automobiles?

We have to recognize that living standards are not merely a function of national income levels. They are bound by the limited natural resources available within a nation's borders. India's population density is nine times that of the US. Hence the average Indian can never enjoy the 2,500 square foot single-family home with front and back yards, which is so commonplace in American suburbia. Indians may think that they will be able to buy a bigger home if their income rises. But if the average income in a city or region doubles, the price of good housing often more than doubles.

It isn't just housing that's resource-constrained. Clean water and energy are very finite resources, at least in the foreseeable future. To achieve a living standard comparable to the West, Indians will need access to much more fresh water and electricity per capita. India's water situation is precariously dependent on the monsoon even at the current levels of consumption. As for electricity, India's massive fossil-fuel dependence throws it between the devil (of pollution from coal-fired plants) and the deep blue sea (of high oil prices and coming oil shortages).

The bottom line is that money earned from offshoring cannot significantly raise the living conditions of the average Indian, but it definitely raises expectations. The yawning lifestyle gap between the small, techno-savvy class and the rest, simply creates resentment and frustration, not progress.

Technologies Needed to Improve India's Standard of Living

Despite its population and limited natural resources, India is not doomed to poverty and shortage. If India's awesome collective brainpower is directed toward developing and utilizing technologies and strategies appropriate to India, it could dramatically raise its own living standards and that of much of the world. The areas of intense focus should be:

(a) Renewable, low-polluting energy sources: India should be investing a lot more in the development and deployment of solar, wind and waste-biomass power. Consider solar power. Being a tropical country it gets much more solar power per square meter per year than Europe or Japan. Moreover, since Indians have not become "used to" central air-conditioning, even current levels of solar-panel efficiency generate enough electricity for the average Indian home. Or consider hybrid (gas-electric) automobile technology. Given its huge oil-import bill, India should be concentrating on research and development (R&D) and manufacturing of hybrids or fuel-cell technology instead of taking pride in the explosion of gas-guzzling foreign car models on Indian roads.

(b) Water purification and conservation technologies: Most Indian rivers have undrinkable water because raw, untreated sewage is dumped into them by towns and villages upstream. Sewage treatment is not a "sexy" technology, but it is far more important to India's well-being than software or automobiles. Most Indians have neither toilets nor showers. But the fortunate few who do are unaware or unconcerned with installing devices such as low-flow shower heads or dual-action flush tanks.

(c) Biotechnology and pharmaceuticals are making great progress in India, but how little of it is oriented toward the diseases that affect the poor majority of Indians. India doesn't need better cholesterol-fighting drugs. It needs vaccines against malaria, cheap medicines against dysentery, cures for intestinal parasites. But most of all India needs cheaper and simpler contraceptives. If India's population growth is not controlled, the current economic boom will make no long-term difference whatsoever.

Unfortunately, India's dynamic private-sector companies are doing very little in the areas mentioned above. Instead, the lure of foreign investment and the great offshore services boom have them focused on products and competencies that serve wealthy, consumerist Western markets. After struggling to gain political independence after 150 years of colonial rule, India is "willingly" surrendering its economic independence to the agendas of Western corporate shareholders.

How Offshoring Puts India into Technological Bondage

The final irony of the offshoring saga is that it is pushing Indian industry headlong into, what I call, the great intellectual property (IP) trap. Indians are swallowing self-serving Western "advice" that "strengthening" IP protections will encourage research and innovation. In truth, the Western patent regime is completely dysfunctional. Huge companies such as IBM and Microsoft are granted thousands of patents each year, not because they have made that many big "intellectual strides", but because the US patent office, deluged with applications, grants patents to minor improvements that are both obvious and trivial. Worse, a large number of "IP law firms" have come out of the woodwork, to profit from aggressively (sometimes abusively) enforcing these patents. Instead of encouraging innovation, this IP regime stifles it because individual inventors and small companies cannot afford expensive lawyers to defend themselves against predatory patent litigation.

Since R&D in developing economies such as India, China, Brazil and others, is often five to 20 years behind the "cutting edge", almost anything developed independently in these countries will run afoul of some Western patent. If the developing world honors all the patents filed in Western countries, its precious resources will be sucked dry paying royalties, or it will remain in permanent technological bondage. (Look at it from another angle—how much in royalties did the Western world pay India for inventing the zero?) Indians know in their hearts that IP protection is a game stacked in the developed world's favor. They know that no country becomes a great power while playing by some other great powers' rules.

But the CEOs and chairmen of India's budding companies—the Wipros, the Infosys, the Ranbaxys—are not going to speak up in India's interests because they fear that would be the end of their "partnerships" with Western multinationals. How could Indian Business Process Outsourcing (BPO) firms bid for offshore contracts from GE or Intel, if they don't sign on the dotted line with regard to intellectual property?

And what happens when they win the BPO contracts? Thousands of smart, educated Indians then become the intellectual slaves of a foreign company, for a fraction of the wages they pay their own employees. Every line of software code, every engineering drawing, every new molecule, every revolutionary idea now becomes the property of a Western corporation. Naturally, these advances will be duly patented or copyrighted. The supreme irony will be that future generations of Indians will be forking over royalties to Americans or Europeans for the intellectual output of their own countrymen. And that will be offshoring's enduring "legacy" to India.

Periodical Bibliography

The following articles have been selected to supplement the diverse views presented in this chapter.

Jayshree Bajoria	"Crisis in Kashmir," Council on Foreign Relations, September 11, 2008.
Sumit Ganguly and Kanti Bajpai	"Secession Dreams," *Newsweek*, September 3, 2008.
Neeta Lal	"India's Outsourcing Blues," *Asia Sentinel*, May 6, 2008.
Romy Misra	"Outsourcing: Bad for India, Good for US," *Battalion*, October 6, 2008.
Jason Motlagh	"Has War Worn Itself Out in Kashmir?" *San Francisco Chronicle*, May 9, 2008.
Bruce Nussbaum	"Will India and China Destroy the Planet Through Global Warming—Or Save the Planet by Forcing the West to Reduce Carbon Emissions?" *Business Week*, January 24, 2008.
Peter Schumacher, as told to Tarun Narayan	"Indian Offshore Firms Are Game-Changers in Europe," *Indian Management*, August 2006.
Lucy Siegle	"Why Cut Emissions if India's Are on the Up?" *Observer*, November 26, 2006.
Nicholas Stern	"Economics Must Be at the Heart of Any Discussion of How to Fight Climate Change," *Boston Review*, January–February 2007.
Thaindian News	"India Can Lead World Fight Against Climate Change: Al Gore," March 15, 2008.

What Are India's Most Serious Crises?

Chapter Preface

In March 2005, two teenaged girls from poor families in West Bengal, India, committed suicide. They had battled hunger for years and had eaten nothing for several days before choosing to end their lives. As food prices rise, stories such as these are becoming too common. In one case, a young Indian survived twenty days without food before he died. One woman in Uttar Pradesh says that over a period of a year and a half, five of her family members starved to death. Among those who live with hunger, there is a great risk of sickness, disease, and death from conditions that are not normally life threatening. Children are particularly imperiled; their growing bodies need proper nourishment that they cannot get from just the rice, salt, and occasional boiled greens that many families use to subsist. Nearly half of Indian youngsters—a staggering 60 million—are malnourished. Some experts point to this as evidence that hunger and malnutrition are at crisis levels in the country.

It was with these statistics in mind that Vijay Prakash, the principal secretary of the Welfare Department of the state of Bihar, tendered a gutsy proposal in August 2008. He suggested that his people hunt and eat rats. Though some poor, low-caste Indians already do, Prakash wants to turn it into a delicacy that would appeal to most everyone and be served at restaurants, hotels, and train stations. According to him, the plan would work twofold. First, it would help battle hunger and malnutrition. "The beauty is that we have billions of rats," he points out. "Rats have almost no bones and are quite rich in nutrition." Eating rats would also reduce the country's dependence on rice, a grain that's in short supply. The other goal is to combat the rodents that have raided and depleted nearly half of the country's store of grains. Encouraging villagers to catch rats, Prakash reasons, would quell such losses.

The people would also be given incentive to start rat farms, which would generate income for them.

For the most part, Prakash's suggestion was met with disdain. Many people are disgusted by rodents and are wary of diseases rats carry. In much of the world and in most Indian cities, there is a social stigma attached to eating rats that could obstruct this plan. Moreover, some pundits are outraged that rat eating was endorsed by a government official. Raj Patel, author of *Stuffed and Starved*, argues that the suggestion signifies the government's readiness to give up on fighting poverty and hunger. He calls it "a sign of defeat."

As of yet, no proposed solution to India's hunger crisis has gained widespread support. As the next chapter demonstrates, agreement regarding other environmental, social, and religious issues that may be threatening India is just as difficult to reach. Determining what issues should receive top focus requires the insight of many informed parties with opposing interests and views.

"Today, most women, particularly if their husbands don't use condoms, elect sterilization after the second or third child."

Family Limits Are an Effective Way to Reduce India's Population Explosion

Robert Marquand

In this viewpoint, Robert Marquand looks at the southwestern Indian state of Kerala, and finds that it is much different from the rest of India. Kerala has a much lower birth rate than other states in India, and also has a much higher literacy rate among village girls. Many women in Kerala elect to be sterilized after two or three children, although it is completely voluntary, and are offered compensation after the procedure. The lowering of population growth in Kerala has led to increased education and opportunities for women and children. Marquand is a staff writer for The Christian Science Monitor.

As you read, consider the following questions:

1. When is India expected to become the world's most populous nation?

2. What is the literacy rate for village girls in Kerala?

3. In Kerala, how many children do women over 50 have?

As the world hypothetically tops 6 billion people today, about 4.8 billion of them live in developing countries. India alone reached 1 billion last August [1999] and is expected to pass China as the world's most populous nation within 50 years.

Yet in the southwestern Indian state of Kerala, something remarkably different is happening. In this place of palm-tree thickets, jasmine scents, and a library in every town, the population growth rate is nearly flat.

Partly Kerala's rate is due to a history of Christian missionary schooling for all castes, and partly to a progressivist communist government that since 1957 has pushed land reform and education as an answer to every ill.

But mainly, say experts, it is a self-conscious awareness of the value and role of women, and their rights within the family—even in rural areas, where women usually have the least power.

Talk to almost any young woman here, single or married, and the answer is the same: "If you have too many kids, you can't spend enough time educating them," says A. Kumari, who will be wedded on Oct. 20 [2000]. "I don't want a big family."

"I like children but I only want two," says N.P. Asa, a young lawyer whose parents are coconut and nutmeg farmers. "The man I marry will understand this."

Such views explain why Kerala in 1999 has achieved a birth rate that the World Health Organization set for it years ago as a target for 2015.

The contrast with much of India could not be greater. In the feudal northern state of Rajasthan, for example, where village girls are often married at age 14, the birth rate is about six children per family. In Kerala, where women now marry in their 20s, the birth rate is about 2.4. The literacy rate for Rajasthan village girls is less than 10 percent according the United Nations. In Kerala, which educates all classes and castes, about 85 percent of even village girls can read and write, the highest rate in India; it is not unusual to see women laborers reading newspapers on the porch before they head to the fields.

Kerala also has the lowest rates of female infanticide in India, and today women here outnumber men by a factor of roughly 10 to 7.

Kerala women activists point to many problems in the state—rising prostitution, ongoing violence against women, and a general conservatism that limits their mobility. Women, for example, (as in many parts of India) will not freely travel outside after dark.

Yet the "culture of learning" has also led to an anomalous number of "firsts" in India among Kerala women: the first woman Indian Supreme Court justice, the first female head of the stock market, the first state chief engineer, the first surgeon general, the first female international literary figure (Arundhati Roy).

In commercial centers like New Delhi and Bombay, moreover, employers advertise for Kerala women—their skill levels and independence are highly valued. Unusual for India as well, Kerala women are willing to travel to distant cities to work, whether or not they are married.

Change the Culture, or Deliver the Goods?

For years, debates on population control have swung between "cultural" and "delivery" factors. Is it more important to focus on education, infrastructure, and building a social agreement

India's Population Projections (in millions)

Year	Under 15 years old	Ages 15–64	Over 65	Total
2000	361	604	45	1010
2005	368	673	51	1093
2010	370	747	58	1175
2015	372	819	65	1256
2020	373	882	76	1331

TAKEN FROM: Compiled using statistics from P.N. Mari Bhat, "Indian Demographic Scenario 2025," Institute of Economic Growth, 2001.

of low growth? Or should emphasis be on contraceptive distribution, family-planning clinics, and word-of-mouth programs?

"In 1974, people were saying 'Development is the best contraceptive,' and even today you have leaders saying that just educating women is enough," says Michael Vlassof, a demographer with the UN Population Fund in New Delhi. "Today we know that strategy by itself works only very slowly. If a woman has to slog through muddy roads all day to get contraceptives, it doesn't matter how much education she has."

In some ways, Kerala is an example of both factors at work. The isolated coastal state has a long history of trade and interaction with African and European cultures and thinking. There is an in-built assumption of progress and openness. The state is 20 percent Muslim, 20 percent Christian, and 60 percent Hindu. Last year [1999] a Muslim girl, for the first time, scored the highest of all students on the state high school exam.

"In north India, there is a strong belief in fate, and the passive acceptance of fate, that you don't find here," says Ignatius Gonsalves, bureau chief of the state newspaper *Malayala Manoram*.

Mr. Gonsalves, whose ancestors were Portuguese missionaries, says in Kerala "People have dreams and believe they can achieve them—it is an atmosphere of progress and cultural diversity. Our last communal riot was in the early 1970s." (Muslim-Hindu riots were common during much of the 1990s, and the past 15 months have seen a rise of Hindu-fundamentalist violence against Christians in India.)

In the 1960s, when the local communist government decided early to make population an issue, partly to create an educated class for economic value, there was an agreement to widely distribute contraceptives. The road system in Kerala was helpful; most people here live on the narrow stretch of land between the coast and the Western Ghat mountains. Most villages, also part of the land reforms of the 1950s, have populations of about 5,000, and unlike smaller villages in other parts of India, have post offices, schools, and other municipal buildings.

Women Activists' Role

The low-growth program was widely successful, appealing to the state's "rationalist" traditions: If Kerala goes the way of the rest of India, it will be poorer and poorer, and the living standard will fall.

"Look, everyone believes that now," says Gonsalves. "It has been internalized, and today no one has to run around preaching about population."

At about the same time, women activists also took up the challenge. Many women over 50 here have three to five children. But a word-of-mouth campaign, and free health services, changed the dynamics. Today, most women, particularly if their husbands don't use condoms, elect sterilization after the second or third child. Both women and men in Kerala are offered a small sum for being sterilized, though the procedure is voluntary. A forced sterilization program for men in the late

1970s, under the sway of Prime Minister Indira Gandhi's son Sanjay, is considered to be one of modern India's darkest hours.

Typical of the Keralite female education is a learning festival held each semester at the women's St. Teresa's College. Women age 15 to 22 would compete for the best performance, art, or essay on subjects such as population growth, women's exploitation, female infanticide, pollution, and resource depletion in India.

"One of our biggest areas of real learning are the youth festivals that take up issues of women, antidrug use, and child labor," says Maggie Artchasery, a quick-witted English instructor at St. Teresa's, which has been one of the most respected women's colleges in Cochin since it was founded in the early 1920s. About 20 percent of St. Teresa's students are tribals or Dalits ("untouchables" [outcastes]), about 20 percent are Christians, and the rest tend to be Hindus of other castes.

"Keralites as a whole tend to be people who cross borders and boundaries and come home with a very wide perspective," says Ms. Artchasery. "We open up and go around the world, and bring home the lessons we've learned. It's one of the reasons the women here are more aware."

| "These policies employ disturbing new incentives and disincentives that trample on the rights and health of the country's people."

Two-Child Limits in India Bring Devastating Consequences

Rajani Bhatia

Rajani Bhatia is a women's rights activist and member of the Committee on Women, Population and the Environment. In the viewpoint that follows, she insists that measures to limit Indian families to no more than two children have harmful consequences. In her contention, programs that offer incentives and disincentives for population control violate rights, cause socio-economic and political disparities, and lead to forced abortions and child abandonment. Such measures, according to Bhatia, adversely impact women and people of lower castes the most.

As you read, consider the following questions:

1. In Bhatia's view, what caused alarmism around the need to control India's population?

Rajani Bhatia, "Ten Years After Cairo: The Resurgence of Coercive Population Control in India," *DifferenTakes*, Spring 2005. Copyright © 2008 DifferenTakes Population and Development Program, Hampshire College. Reproduced by permission.

2. Name five methods people used to evade electoral disincentive laws, according to the United Nations study cited in the viewpoint.

3. What exploitation does the author claim occurred under the guns-for-sterilization scheme?

In 1994 at the U.N. [United Nations] International Conference on Population and Development (ICPD) in Cairo [Egypt], world leaders reached a new consensus on population. Although the ICPD Program of Action (POA) legitimizes demographic goals set by national governments, it recommends policy approaches based on the promotion of reproductive health, informed free choice, and gender equity. The document specifically rejects the use of coercion in family planning programs and discourages the use of social and economic incentives and disincentives to reduce fertility.

However, today after commemorations of the tenth anniversary of the ICPD have taken place around the world, population control is still with us. While the negative effects of China's one-child policy have received much attention, recent two-child norm policies in India have also had devastating consequences for women and the poor. It is important that women's health and reproductive rights activists remain vigilant about the continuing impact of population control.

The Creation of Two-Child Norm Policies

During the last 15 years, population control in India has moved away from a tightly connected system of policies imposed by the central government mainly involving pressure on the poor to be sterilized. Instead, individual states are devising their own schemes to enforce a two-child norm. Designed to deter parents of two children from having a third, these policies employ disturbing new incentives and disincentives that trample on the rights and health of the country's people. Disincentive penalties prohibit parents of more than two children from holding posts in local village councils or seeking government employment and deny or circumscribe access to public provision of education, health insurance and other welfare benefits. Working in the reverse, new forms of incentives give preferential access to anti-poverty and employment schemes to individuals who accept sterilization after two children. Emerging studies show how these population control policies have increased socio-economic and political disparities as well as gender-based violence in the country.

Oddly, most of the two-child norm policies came about either concurrent to or just after the national government of India made significant policy changes consistent with the ICPD Program of Action. First, a Target Free Approach (TFA) was adopted in April 1996, which officially removed targets related to contraceptive acceptance. In February 2000 the government announced a new National Population Policy (NPP 2000) that upheld the principles of voluntarism and informed consent in reproductive health care provision. However, many of the new strategies never had a chance to get off paper and on the ground. Health Watch, a watchdog coalition formed to monitor the government's commitments made in Cairo, conducted surveys in nine states and found the new approach poorly implemented. In those areas where the TFA was tried, many officials doubted its merits and too quickly interpreted the subsequent fall in sterilization rates as system failure.

When India's population crossed the one billion mark on May 11, 2000, alarmism around the need to reduce population further undid what little progress had been made toward upholding ICPD and NPP principles in state health policies. M.K. Raut, a government official from Chattisgarh state, for example, expressed this common sentiment, "We can't wait forever. The empowerment route advocated by the Cairo declaration is a long process and we would have added another billion by then . . . Yes, it is coercion. But with a billion-plus people, family size is no longer a personal matter." The current national government led by the newly elected Congress Party has thus far taken no action to pressure states into adhering to NPP 2000 principles. As recently reported by the *Washington Post*, officials of the Indian Ministry of Health and Family Welfare describe population issues as an area now mandated by states without central regulation.

How Electoral Laws Create Political Disparity

Among the most controversial disincentives are electoral laws that since 1992 have sprung up in eight states. These debar anyone with more than two children from holding office in local government bodies or village councils known as *panchayats*. As a result over 4000 *panchayat* members have been forced to vacate their posts upon having a third child. State officials say they devised electoral disincentive laws in order to force village council members to act as role models in encouraging smaller families.

In July 2003 the Supreme Court of India gave a national stamp of approval to the state two-child norm policies by upholding the constitutionality of the electoral disincentive law of Haryana state. In its ruling the Supreme Court stated, "Disqualification on the right to contest an election for having more than two children does not contravene any fundamental right, nor does it cross the limits of reasonability. Rather, it is a disqualification conceptually devised in the national interest." Emphasizing India's "burgeoning population" as a national problem causing everything from congestion in urban areas to shortfalls in food grains and reduced per capita income, the Supreme Court further observed, "Complacence in controlling population in the name of democracy is too heavy a price to pay, allowing the nation to drift towards disaster." Critics of the two-child norm and the Supreme Court decision have likened current policies to the 1970s Emergency Period in India's political history remembered for massive forced sterilizations and suspension of democratic rights.

A study conducted by the Bhopal-based NGO [non-governmental organization], Mahila Chetna Manch, between July 2001 and March 2002 clearly reveals how state policies have adversely impacted local communities and their village councils. Commissioned by the Ministry of Health and Family Welfare with support from the U.N. Fund for Population Activities (UNFPA), the study covered the states of Andhra Pradesh, Maharashtra, Madhya Pradesh, Orissa and Rajasthan. It found that 75 percent of those disqualified from their *panchayat* posts for having a third child belonged to economically and socially disadvantaged groups known as Scheduled Castes and Tribes. People resorted to a variety of means in order to evade the law including forced abortion, desertion of pregnant wives, divorce, extra-marital affairs, denial of paternity, hiding babies or children (for example by not allowing them to attend school), child abandonment, tampering of birth and immunization records, and giving away of children in adoption. The laws also resulted in a marked rise in the number of prenatal sex determination tests and abortion of female fetuses. In the case of a male fetus, most mothers were pressured into having a third child with the consequence of losing her own or her husband's post in the *panchayat*.

Sterilization Bribes

Meanwhile, the traditional system of incentives has not disappeared entirely. In the state of Andhra Pradesh, for example, Health Watch documented the use of gold chains to entice women to get sterilized after having two children. States have also employed a range of new incentives to allow individuals accepting sterilization preferential access to subsidized housing, food, government jobs and the like. In addition, some states have implemented group or community incentive schemes that give preferential access to development grants

Powerful Elected Leaders Dodge the Two-Child Norm While Others Are Punished

There are Panchayat Raj-level elected leaders who have well more than two children but who have never been approached to step down from their seat because they are connected enough to avoid the teeth of the policy. Meanwhile, the low caste and low income women, Dalits, and adivasis serving for the first time in government—and whose leadership is so badly needed to represent the needs of their communities—are almost exclusively the people who are removed from their hard-fought seats. . . . There are numerous cases of elected officials using the Two-Child Norm policy as a means of threatening political opponents and exacting revenge against other representatives who disagree with their platforms and/or agendas.

Claire Cole, "Coercive Population Policy in India: a Fine 'Howdy-Do,'" Feministe, July 22, 2008. www.feministe.us.

for housing, sanitation, school buildings, etc., based on collective family planning performance. As in the past, Madhya Pradesh, Andhra Pradesh and Maharashtra provide performance awards to service providers who meet family planning targets.

Most shocking is a guns-for-sterilization scheme put into place in three districts of Uttar Pradesh. The policy mirrors past incentives for family planning "motivators," but is directed at harnessing the exploitive power of rich, land-owning farmers. Bringing in two people for sterilization gets you a single-barrel shotgun; five people a revolver license. The London *Guardian* recently reported a case of five poor farmers who in July 2004 were lured by a rich farmer's offer of work and then forcibly sterilized.

Some states employ population policies to address social issues such as low age at marriage, son preference and lack of male responsibility in contraception—but unfortunately by punitive or preferential means. Uttar Pradesh, Rajasthan and Madhya Pradesh, for example, deny individuals married before the legal age of 18 access to government jobs, thereby further disempowering women forced against their will to marry early. Similarly ill-conceived is a policy in Andhra Pradesh that awards three couples selected by a "lucky lotto" dip 10,000 rupees. In order to qualify for the lotto, couples must either adopt a permanent method of family planning after having one child or two girl children or by adopting vasectomy after having one or two children.

Neo-liberal economic and deregulation policies of the past ten to fifteen years have also had a negative effect. Resource allocations to the health sector have fallen at both federal and state levels. The research of Health Watch revealed that many women in India do not have easy access to basic health care or even minimum reproductive health care services. The context of population control has become decentralized as a host of different actors including state and local government bodies, NGOs, corporations, and lending sources for microbusinesses implement separate strategies to instill a two-child norm.

| "As sex-specific abortions increase, the destabilizing effects on Indian society are bound to greatly impact [the] country."

Female Infanticide and Abortion Are India's Biggest Crises

Julia Duin

Infanticide, or feticide, is the killing of babies. In the following viewpoint Julia Duin, religion editor for the Washington Times *and two-time Pulitzer Prize nominee, contends that abortion and feticide of females in India are causing an epic gender gap. There have been 10 million more aborted girls than boys over the past two decades, leaving men without prospective wives, she avers. Duin testifies that females are less valued than males due to long-standing traditions in India that require a woman's family to pay a dowry to her husband when she marries and to be responsible for other costs throughout her lifetime.*

As you read, consider the following questions:

1. In Duin's assertion, when and why did India's boy-girl ratio begin to widen precipitously?

Julia Duin, "India's Imbalance of Sexes," *Washington Times*, February 26, 2007. Copyright © 2007 The Washington Times LLC. Reproduced by permission.

2. How does the author explain the saying, "Better 500 rupees now rather than 50,000 rupees later"?

3. Why has Dr. Tajinder P. Singh been threatened and shunned, according to the viewpoint?

"Raising a daughter is like watering your neighbor's garden."

—*Punjabi saying*

By early afternoon, wedding festivities were well under way for Gagandeep Singh, 29, and Taranjeet Kaur, 26, in this touristy town in the Himalayan foothills of the Indian state of Himachal Pradesh.

Mr. Singh, the groom, works at an American Express office near New Delhi. He is seated cross-legged in a large, gracious white Sikh temple overlooking the Nagar River. His ceremonial finery includes a dagger and ornate turban.

Beside him is his bride, her hands heavily hennaed with designs befitting a newly married woman. She is dressed in a magenta-colored gown and spends much of the ceremony gazing down at the floor. Nestled beside her like a flock of bright birds are female relatives dressed in brilliant jewel-colored tunics known as salwar kameez.

In front of the couple are Sikh priests. They alternately pray, sprinkle holy water on the crowd and instruct the couple to circle around a low-lying altar as a trio of musicians tap out rhythms on tabla drums and a harmonium.

Later, back at the wedding hall, the bride's father, Amarjit Singh, reveals he has given a refrigerator, TV, washing machine, clothes and a DVD player to the family of the groom.

"This is not dowry," he protests, "these are just gifts the father likes to give for his daughter."

Miss Kaur is his only daughter and later that evening, she sits in her family's living room as guest after guest shoves stacks of rupees into her purse. Eventually, a car pulls up containing the groom's family. Wailing and clutching her parents for the last time, she slowly marches toward the waiting car that will bear her 30 miles southward to Yamunanagar, the city where her new husband's family lives.

"Indian brides handle these partings with great theatrics, often wailing uncontrollably," observed American journalist Elisabeth Bumiller in her 1990 book on the trials of Indian women, *May You Be the Mother of a Hundred Sons*.

"I decided this was the only rational response, given what was in store for many of them," she said.

More Boys than Girls

India is facing a shortage of women like Miss Kaur.

In most places in the world, a mother can find out the sex of her unborn child, but in India, it's illegal to do so. That is because if she's a female, there is a good chance she will never be born.

Roughly 6.7 million abortions occur yearly in India, but aborted girls outnumber boys by 500,000—or 10 million over the past two decades—creating a huge imbalance between males and females in the world's largest democracy.

Ratios of men to women are being altered at an unprecedented rate in India and neighboring China, two countries which account for 40 percent of the world's population.

According to UNICEF [the United Nations Children's Fund], India produces 25 million babies a year. China produces 17 million. Together, these are one-third of the world's babies, so how their women choose to regulate births affects the globe.

Female infanticide—whereby tiny girls were either poisoned, buried alive or strangled—has existed for thousands of years in India. But its boy-to-girl ratio didn't begin to widen precipitously until the advent of the ultrasound, or sonogram, machine in the 1970s, enabling a woman to tell the sex of her child by the fourth month of her pregnancy.

That coupled with the legalization of abortion in 1971 made it possible to dispose of an unwanted girl without the neighbors even knowing the mother was pregnant. In 2001, 927 girls were born for every 1,000 boys, significantly below the natural birth rate of about 952 girls for every 1,000 boys.

In many regions, however, this imbalance has reached alarming levels and it continues to grow. In 2004, the New Delhi-based magazine *Outlook* reported, sex ratios in the capital had plummeted to 818 girls for every 1,000 boys, and in 2005 they had slipped to 814.

The issue is highly sensitive for the Indian government, which had given the nation's sex imbalance scant attention until this month [February 2007].

"It is a matter of international and national shame for us that India, with [economic] growth of 9 percent still kills its daughters," Renuka Chowdhury, the Cabinet-level minister of state for women and child development told the Press Trust of India news agency in an interview that was widely published in the national press.

Mrs. Chowdhury announced plans to set up a nationwide network of orphanages where women can drop off unwanted daughters with no questions asked.

"We will bring up the children. But don't kill them because there really is a crisis situation," she says.

Yet the practice of "female feticide" is so widespread and deeply ingrained in the nation's psyche, scholars and activists fear that even the most vigorous attempts to combat it would require a lifetime or longer to restore nature's balance.

"There has always been a deficit of women: Infanticide, neglect or they're left to die if they are sick, but technology has accentuated it," says Prem Chowdhry, a New Delhi-based scholar and specialist on male-female relations in India. "The volume has grown. Culturally, these things are not new, but now they're taking a new shape."

Early this year [2007], the British medical journal *Lancet* estimated the male-female gap at 43 million. Worldwide, *Lancet* said, there are 100 million "missing girls" who should have been born but were not. Fifty million of them would have been Chinese and 43 million would have been Indian. The rest would have been born in Afghanistan, South Korea, Pakistan and Nepal.

China gave an even bleaker assessment last month [January 2007], with the government saying that its men will outnumber women in the year 2020 by 300 million.

One Geneva-based research center, in a 2005 update on the phenomenon, termed it "the slaughter of Eve."

"What we're seeing now is genocide," says Sabu George, a New Delhi-based activist. "We will soon exceed China in losing 1 million girls a year."

The date may already be here. In a report released Dec. 12, UNICEF said India is "missing" 7,000 girls a day or 2.5 million a year.

Although India has passed laws forbidding sex-specific abortions, legions of compliant doctors and lax government officials involved in India's $100 million sex-selection industry have made sure they are rarely enforced.

Several companies, notably General Electric Corp., have profited hugely from India's love affair with the ultrasound machine.

As a result, a new class of wifeless men are scouring eastern India, Bangladesh and Nepal for available women. India, already a world leader in sex trafficking, is absorbing a new trade in girls kidnapped or sold from their homes and shipped across the country.

As sex-specific abortions increase, the destabilizing effects on Indian society are bound to greatly impact a country with expanding economic and strategic ties to the United States.

Programs of the Indian State of Tamil Nadu to Discourage Female Feticide

One [program to protect girls] urged families to hand over their baby girls to local officials, who saw that they were adopted by childless couples. Between May 2001 and January 2003, officials received 361 baby girls. An informal survey by CSG [Community Services Guild], however, found that many women would abort rather than have a baby and give her up for adoption.

Tamil Nadu's "Girl Protection" program may be more practical. Here, the government opens a bank account in a girl's name at her birth, depositing between 15,000 and 22,000 rupees during her childhood, depending on the number of girls in the family.

"The only way to wipe out this evil is by an attitudinal shift," says CSG's Mr. [G.] Prasad. "Educate a girl beyond eighth grade and encourage her to find her voice."

Uma Girish,
Christian Science Monitor, *February 21, 2008.*

India's estimated $23 billion defense budget relies on military hardware from U.S. corporations, and the U.S. Congress voted in November to permit the sale of nuclear technology to the country.

In September [2007], *The Washington Times* sent a reporter and photographer to spend three weeks in different parts of India chronicling this problem. They asked: What are the cultural reasons for this genocide? Why is the government allowing it? Who is fighting against it and what steps can be taken to stop it?

Dowry Deaths

Sister Mary Scaria was one of two girls in a family of nine children.

Dressed in an aqua-colored sari of the Sisters of Charity of Jesus and Mary, the nun is also a lawyer and coordinator of the Delhi Catholic Archdiocese's Justice & Peace Commission. In early 2006, she published *Woman: An Endangered Species?* which charged that "female feticide" is decimating half of the population.

She chiefly blames the dowry system, a Hindu marriage practice by which the groom's family demands enormous sums of money and goods from the bride's family as a condition for letting their son marry her.

"At a wedding, everyone looks to see how many bracelets the bride has and how much gold she has," the nun says. Dowries typically consist of gold and appliances, as well as substantial amounts of cash. Defenders of the system say that girls are often denied an inheritance in India; thus, what she gets at her wedding is in effect a savings account she can retain for the rest of her life.

What actually happens is the groom's family pockets the dowry, the nun explains, and the payments don't stop there.

"When a wife has a baby in India, the wife's family has to pay for the hospital stay," Sister Mary says. "After the birth, they also have to bring gold and food for the new family, even new saris for all the relatives."

Some Indian castes even require that the bride's family pay her funeral expenses when she dies. Worse yet, the groom's family will often kill the bride in what's known as a "dowry death" if they think the dowry is too small.

Many families therefore elect to not have a girl at all. Medical clinics—which Sister Mary calls "womb raiders"— have advertised "better 500 rupees now [for an abortion] rather than 50,000 rupees later" [for a dowry]. The first amount is about $11; the second is $1,100.

Dowries are theoretically banned under the 1961 Dowry Prohibition Act, but enforcement is poor and other religious groups such as Muslims and Christians have been caught up in the custom.

Sister Mary says that if she were to get married, her Catholic family would have to pay up.

A Sept. 29 article in the *Times of India* front-paged its account of a Muslim family in New Delhi that dumped a new daughter-in-law within 24 hours after the wedding because the dowry was not big enough.

The groom said he wanted about $4,400 more "as well as a Pulsar [motor] bike," the bride told the newspaper.

Caste Causes

It's a sultry evening and Ms. Chowdhry, dressed in an olive green salwar kameez, orange pants and gold bracelets, is reflecting on why the life of an Indian woman can be so miserable.

"First," says the New Delhi-based scholar, "girls can get killed for a number of reasons, including anything that brings dishonor. A girl can be killed before she is born. If she survives, she is forcibly married. If there's not enough dowry, she is killed."

She cites the Indian state of Haryana, just north of New Delhi, which has the country's second highest per capita income. It also has India's second worst sex ratio, after Punjab state to the west. For every 1,000 boys born in Haryana, just 820 girls were born, according to the 2001 census. In 1991, it was 879 girls.

Punjab is similarly wealthy; thus, instead of the poor killing their children, it's the rich, says Ms. Chowdhry, a former senior fellow at the Nehru Memorial Institute and Library.

"Punjab and Haryana are the two highest per capita income states, but they have such regressive trends," she says. "How can they call themselves modern?"

India's caste system "is very basic to violence against women," she says. It is based on Hinduism, which teaches one's behavior in this life determines which caste one will be born into for the next life. Individuals are expected to marry within their caste.

Thus, the shortage of girls is a "huge problem" to men in Haryana and Punjab who wish to observe caste practices.

"In Haryana, 36 percent of the men between 15–45 are unmarried," she says. "In one district, it's 40 percent. Men who do not get married get more vicious."

Richer men will be able to get themselves wives; what's troubling to Ms. Chowdhry are the poorer men who are importing brides from India's poor eastern regions.

"These women are extensively sexually exploited," she says. "They do all the housework, manual and field work. Some of these women, once they are used by a man, they are passed on to another."

Pregnant women wishing to avoid having daughters who might suffer such a fate are desperate to find doctors who will tell them the sex of their children.

"Mobile vans have advertisements on them that a doctor is available," Ms. Chowdhry says. "They are innocuous, but everyone knows what's inside."

Sikh Radiologist

The city of Yamunanagar, population 300,000 located 130 miles north of New Delhi, is encircled by wheat and sugar cane fields, bisected by the Yamuna River and dotted with herds of black water buffalo.

The area north of New Delhi has the country's most severe shortages of girls. In Yamunanagar alone, there are 30 doctors who will illegally abort a female child at the request of the parents, says Dr. Tajinder P. Singh, 45, a local radiologist.

He refuses to tell pregnant women the sex of their off-spring after their ultrasound tests in his office in a Yamunanagar strip mall. And he reports the names of those doctors who do to the government.

In response, doctors refuse to refer their patients to him, his family has been physically threatened, and he was thrown out of the local branch of the Indian Medical Association.

Asked how he copes, he says: "My family is small, my house is small, my daughters don't ask for much money."

In New Delhi, one of the city's top obstetricians, Dr. Puneet Bedi, has likewise been blackballed by his associates for his stance against "female feticide."

"I can work only as a visiting consultant and only work at small hospitals," he says sadly. "But that is the price you pay. Feticide is the tip of the iceberg on medical malpractice here.

"Feticide was invented, touted and sold by the medical profession, and it operates with the complete consent of all factors of society," he says.

What keeps him going?

"Oh, nothing," he responds. "A lot of us are quite frustrated. I didn't choose to be an activist. But the amount of malpractice is so bad here—either you get involved in it or you get desensitized to it. I know a lot of good doctors who do not practice it, but they also do not speak against it.

"Of my 10 first cousins in Punjab, no one has had a daughter in 10 years," he says. "You hope someone else would be stupid enough to produce a girl but not you."

"*[Hindu] religiosity has become more active and aggressive with the injection of nationalism.*"

Hindu Nationalism Is a Threat to India

Sharif Shuja

Sharif Shuja is a research associate in the Global Terrorism Research Unit at Australia's Monash University. In the viewpoint that follows, Shuja argues that the religious militancy of some Hindus in India threatens democracy and the entire country. Hindutva is a Hindu nationalist movement that Shuja disparages as aggressive and intolerant. Its followers, he avers, oppose secularism, a defining element of India. Shuja contends that these fundamentalists commit violence against Indian Muslims, promote bigoted views of Muslims, and rewrite history books to make past events in favor of Hinduism.

As you read, consider the following questions:

1. To what does the author attribute the rise of the Hindutva ideology and Bharatiya Janata Party politics?

Sharif Shuja, "Indian Secularism: Image and Reality," *Contemporary Review*, July 1, 2005, p. 38. Copyright © 2005 Contemporary Review Company Ltd. Reproduced by the permission of Contemporary Review Ltd.

2. Name four ways in which history textbooks were altered or rewritten by Hindu nationalists, according to the author.

3. What are three stereotypes held by many conservative Indians towards Muslims, in the author's opinion?

In recent years, religious militancy and communal strife have become the biggest danger to India's secular fabric. Had the Bharatiya Janata Party (BJP) won last year's [the 2004] election, power would probably have gradually shifted into the hands of Hindutva fanatics, who were careful to play down the communal card. The term 'Hindutva' is derived from the two terms *Hindu Tattva*, which literally mean Hindu Principles, aimed at promoting Hindu unity. But there is a distinction between Hinduism and Hindutva. Such a distinction is important because the latter, Hindutva, has a history of blood letting—from the murder of Mahatma Gandhi (killed by a Hindutva ideologue, Nathuram Godse) to the more than 20,000 lives claimed in communal violence in India since 1950.

Hindutva is a nationalist ideology, based on a modern-day version of centralised intolerant Hinduism. Such a centralised and chauvinistic Hinduism—Hindutva—has been brought to the forefront today by a group of political organisations called the 'Sangh Parivar' (Sangh family)—consisting of the Rashtriya Swayamsevak Sangh (RSS), the Bharatiya Janata Party (BJP), the Vishwa Hindu Parishad (VHP) and the Shiv Sena (the fascist front). Hindutva did not go down well with the voters in the 2004 Indian elections. Explanations for the BJP debacle vary; but one thing is clear—its effort to mould a national ethos that would reflect the ideology of Hindutva has failed miserably.

A defining element of Indian politics since independence has been a commitment to secularism. India, although predominantly Hindu, is a secular state, but it has to deal with the 'problem of Islam' and the Muslims. Muslims in India are persecuted every now and then. The cultural clash is not between the traditional, rural Hindus and Muslims, but the modern, urban ones. The 'modern Hindu' likes to distinguish himself from the Muslim, who is often blamed, along with his heritage and history, for being a problem in society. Such a trend is more visible in the conservative factions of Hindu society than among followers of the BJP. The BJP is a nationalist party which equates Indian national identity with Hindu religious identity. The country's radical nationalists view the secular political system as a threat to Hindu identity, largely because of the power it allows to India's 140 million Muslims. Weakening, or even abolishing, the secular state has therefore become part of the radical nationalist agenda.

This may force Indian Muslims—traditionally moderate and supportive of the secular state, even on the sensitive matter of Kashmir[1]—to shift their allegiance from the state to some sort of large international Islamic movement, as many Muslims have done in Indonesia, Malaysia, and Singapore. Such a radicalisation of religious identities is a matter of serious concern in a nation of a billion people that possesses a nuclear arsenal and has had troubled relations with its populous and nuclear-armed Muslim neighbour, Pakistan.

Destruction and Massacres

Radical Hindu nationalism is a dominant form in mainstream Indian politics. The BJP is a nationalist party whose goal is to convert India into a Hindu nation. The Hindus are profoundly religious, but this religiosity has become more active and aggressive with the injection of nationalism. The ideology of the BJP threatens not only democracy but the unity of India itself. Its most violent elements were responsible for destroying the historic 430-year-old Babri mosque in the small city of Ayodhya in the northern Indian state of Uttar Pradesh. On De-

1. Kashmir is a disputed region shared by Pakistan and India.

cember 6, 1992, a mob of 300,000 fanatics, brought together by the BJP and other extreme right-wing groups, demolished the mosque and promptly built a shrine dedicated to Rama. Hindus believed the site to be the birthplace of Ram, an incarnation of the god Vishnu. But the Muslim place of worship was a nationally recognised symbol of the secularism guaranteed by India's democratic constitution. The result was a series of riots in which more than 1,500 people, largely Muslims, died.

Similarly the BJP turned a blind eye to attacks on the Gujarat Muslim minority that killed about 2,000 people in March 2002. An Indian tribunal investigating the massacres found that Hindu nationalist groups had methodically targeted Muslim homes and shops. Local and national security forces failed to respond adequately to the crisis as it unfolded. Initially the state police did not intervene, and the central government only belatedly sent troops to Gujarat to restore order.

On the whole, the Gujarat episode left Indian Muslims feeling neglected by the government. It also destabilised the Vajpayee-led coalition government whose hard-line policies became increasingly unpopular with the 21 coalition partners, the media and civil organisations. The communal riots in Gujarat alone cost the nation millions of dollars not only in property damage, but also in lost productive time (grief, injury and stress causing underproduction), recovery costs (treatment, loss of experience, retraining of new incumbents) and other costs (legal, administrative and social). It was a horrendous crime committed on a mass scale. Its perpetrators must be punished because crimes unpunished generate more criminals.

Explaining the Rise in Hindu Nationalism

The ascendancy of the Hindutva ideology and of BJP politics is partly attributable to the upward mobility of the middle-class, and to an extent, the property-owning middle-castes. Its ascendancy has led to a burgeoning middle-class with rising consumption, which is seriously alienated from the people, and secondarily, to a business elite that is highly predatory. This middle-class ascendancy occurred in particular circumstances—the rise of ethnic-religious identity politics in India's neighbourhood, and intensified India-Pakistan rivalry. Therefore, it came with a heavy baggage of chauvinist-nationalism and militarism. The BJP was the greatest beneficiary of this nationalism.

Militants associated with the larger Hindu movement, such as the *Rashtriya Swayamsevak Sangh* (RSS), are intolerant of members of lower castes and non-Hindus. They are opposed to Indian secularism and make no secret of wanting a common culture called Hindutva that all Indians, whatever their religion or background, would be required to accept. To appease them, the BJP-led government changed text books and courses in schools and colleges to emphasise the past glories of Hinduism.

Rewriting History

The former BJP-led government made the writing of history a high-profile political issue. The BJP's initiative was to change history. Hence, the paradigm was relentlessly shifted from the secular to the communal—Murli Manohar Joshi being the chief architect of the enterprise. Murli was Minister for Human Resources and Development. One of his main acts was to reconstitute the Indian Council of Historical Research (ICHR), filling it with Sangh sympathisers. Secondly, the Council was required to review documents from the national archives for the years running up to 1947. Among the documents suppressed by the ICHR were statements by Hindu nationalists indicating ambivalence in their support for the freedom movement—a part of the historical record that might undermine the Sangh's patriotic credentials.

This attack is essentially rooted in a fear of history, and that fear arises from the fact that these volumes present a documentary record which cannot be denied. In 2000, Joshi's ministry issued a new National Curriculum Framework for School Education calling for greater emphasis on ancient India's achievements and 'sustaining and emphasising the indigenous knowledge ingrained in the Indian tradition'.

Following guidance from Joshi's ministry the National Council of Educational Research and Training (NCERT) ordered deletions in a number of history text books. The deleted passages included references to beef-eating among ancient Indians [which is prohibited in Hinduism]; the textual evolution over centuries of Sanskrit epics, the *Mahabharata* and the *Ramayana*; Brahmin antipathy to the Buddhist king, Asoka; and the origins and development of caste society.

This was followed by the commissioning, and in 2002 the publication of a new range of history texts. To the dismay of many in the profession, these volumes were littered with errors and infused with a strong Hindutva slant. A report on the textbooks issued by the Indian History Congress, South Asia's largest forum of professional historians, catalogues hundreds of factual errors and examples of distortion.

The new texts adhere to the Hindutva insistence that the Aryans (and by implication their upper-caste Hindu descendants) were the original Indians and that their Vedic culture was entirely indigenous to India. The text equates the Indus Valley or Harappan civilisation with the Vedic—a claim which is strongly contested by most scholars in the field. Ancient India is also described as the original home of mathematics, astronomy and medicine.

On the subject of the medieval period, the new text emphasises the destruction of temples by Muslim rulers, but largely omits the atrocities committed by Hindu rulers. Any regime headed by Muslims is portrayed as an example of 'foreign domination'. The mutual influence of Hindu and Islamic art and thought is denied. In the account of the Mughal Emperor Akbar, there is no mention of his liberal social policies, his prohibition of the slave trade and of involuntary *sati* (widow burning). Similarly, when it comes to the modern era, the new text praises the leaders of the Hindu Mahasabha—predecessors of the BJP—but presents the resolutely secular [first prime minister Jawaharlal] Nehru in an unfavourable light. The great Indian social reform movements that challenged the status of women and lower-caste people are not mentioned, nor is the fact that Nathuram Godse, Gandhi's assassin, was an RSS associate.

Is it the function of history to ignore all unpleasant facts and become a collection of fables or happy tales? Why did the BJP government want to rewrite history? 'History of a particular kind is vital for the Sangh Parivar to consolidate its claim to be the sole spokesman of the Hindus, who have to be convinced that their interests and emotions are, and have always been, unitary and inevitably opposed to those of Muslims or Christians, regardless of differences of caste, gender, class, immense regional variation', said Sumit Sarkar, a former professor of history at Delhi University, 'and BJP'S doctoring of history is an attempt to turn the clock back and if possible do away with history altogether'.

The BJP's Response to Criticism and Defeat

In January 2004, mobs wreaked havoc at Pune's Bhandarkar Oriental Research Institute because a scholar working there had been acknowledged in a book (*Shivaji: Hindu King in Islamic India*) by James W. Laine, an American academic who allegedly defamed their hero, Shivaji, the seventeenth-century warrior-king who took on the Mughal empire and founded the Maratha Confederacy.

The book is a study of the legends and traditions surrounding the pre-eminent Maratha hero. The book caused outrage among Hindu nationalists and was later banned by

Minority Religious Groups Face Persecution in India

The BJP [Bharatiya Janata Party] advances the ideology of Hindutva through propaganda, the manipulation of cultural institutions, undercutting laws that protect religious minorities, and minimizing or excusing Hindu extremist violence. . . .

BJP lawmakers have also attempted to restrict minority religious groups' international contacts and to reduce their rights to build places of worship. It works to pass anti-conversion laws and to alter the personal laws that govern marriages, adoptions, and inheritance. It practices legal discrimination against Dalits ("untouchables") who are Christian and Muslim, but not against those who are Hindu. With BJP support, laws have recently been adopted in Tamil Nadu and Gujarat states that restrict the ability of Hindus to change their religion, and proposals for national restrictions have been made.

Paul Marshall, First Things, *June–July 2004.*

the Maharashtra state government. While the Pune incident seems to have been prompted by a local caste-based group, its context is a national one—a public battle over the interpretation of Indian history and the historical method itself. This happened during the BJP-led government.

It is noted that, though the BJP suffered an unexpected defeat in the 2004 elections, they were quick to mount a counter-offensive against the victor, the Italian-born Congress leader Sonia Gandhi, claiming that her 'foreign origins' made her unacceptable as India's prime minister. The foundations for this aggressive campaign had been well laid by the Sangh's version of Indian history, in which Hindutva definitions of indigenous and alien were promoted as absolute.

Many conservatives, especially BJP sympathisers, believe Indian Muslims are backward, illiterate, overly religious, bigoted and resistant to change, especially in matters of dress, customs, and personal laws. In their view, Muslims are somewhat inferior, under-socialised human beings who deserve pity or sympathy, not equal treatment or respect. The Hindunationalist as well as the middle-class pseudo-liberal is deeply uncomfortable with the modern, liberal, educated, well-informed Muslim who has an open mind and cosmopolitan outlook. The discomfort is all the greater if the person is a woman. . . .

Secularism Is Crucial

The future of India lies in modernisation, and reform based on the values of the Enlightenment. These values should be promoted in personal as well as public life. Only thus can India become tolerant of, and comfortable with, differences—a society that's truly pluralist and secular.

The new United Progressive Alliance (UPA) government's priority is to uphold and strengthen the secular principles embodied in the Indian Constitution. As India has always been a multi-cultural, multi-ethnic, multi-religious society, secular government is not an option but an absolute necessity. Only secularism, with its emphasis on equality and universal citizenship rights, can build a minimally civilised, inclusive, democratic society and ensure equal rights for all citizens, regardless of religion, ethnicity or culture. Secularism must be practised and advocated vigorously.

> *"Outside the tent here in Allahabad, pilgrims voice their support for this brand of Hindu politics, particularly on the Ram temple issue."*

Hindu Nationalism Has a Place in Indian Politics

Scott Baldauf

In this viewpoint, Scott Baldauf discusses the relationship between politics and Hinduism in India. Hindu nationalists use religious festivals, such as the Kumbh Mela, to reach devout Hindu voters and drum up support, which breaks with the past. These Hindu pilgrims also have a chance to express their concerns and make demands on the government. Baldauf is a staff writer for The Christian Science Monitor.

As you read, consider the following questions:

1. What is the Kumbh Mela festival?

2. What happened to previous attempts to politicize the Kumbh Mela festival?

3. What sets Indian politics apart from American politics?

In the frigid fog of daybreak, millions of pilgrims make their way to the juncture of three rivers, the Ganges, the Jamuna, and the mythical underground Saraswati, all in hopes of washing away their sins.

For centuries, this two-month-long Hindu festival called the Kumbh Mela has attracted Indians of all castes, questioners, and faithful alike.

But this year [2001], the Kumbh has taken on a political tone, with politicians and muckrakers wrapping themselves in the saffron cloth of Hinduism to reach devout Hindu voters.

Call it the politics of bathing, but don't call it an entirely welcome trend.

"This is the first time the Kumbh has been used as a vehicle for narrow political purposes," says Amitabh Mattoo, a political scientist at Jawaharlal Nehru University in New Delhi. "But Hinduism is so pluralistic, with so many different schools, so many gods, so many practices and modes of thought, that it would be very difficult for anyone to try to slot it into one box."

Even after the devastating earthquake in Gujarat two weeks ago [January 2001] which largely halted all other festivities around the country, the Kumbh must go on. And with an estimated 70 million pilgrims—an attendance almost the size of the German population, gathering for the Jan. 9 to Feb. 21 festival, this year's Kumbh makes an irresistible target for political opportunists.

But it also illustrates the difficulty of moving this vast, pluralistic country in one direction.

In fact, some say the Kumbh is a metaphor for Hinduism itself: The meeting place of many divergent streams of thought, with a common faith but conflicting goals.

A Mythical Appeal

To understand why so many people come here—including Western rock stars and Hollywood celebrities, it helps to get a quick primer on Hindu mythology.

According to ancient texts, the gods and the demons joined forces to churn the sea and bring up the elixir of eternal life. This elixir was gathered in a kumbh, or earthen pot, and drops of the elixir fell to the earth, landing in four places. One of those was the city now called Allahabad.

A Hindu king in the 1500s started taking his bath here every 12 years to commemorate the event.

Out of this regular ritual has grown the Kumbh Mela.

No Escape from Politics

Today's Kumbh is part tent-revival meeting, part campout, and part polar bear swim club. But for most of history, it was purely a religious festival, untouched by the storm and fury of Indian politics.

Attempts to politicize it often turned out to be duds. Take the late 19th century freedom fighter Bal Gangadhar Tilak, for instance, who once tried to use the Kumbh to mobilize Hindus against British rule. Meanwhile, his contemporary, Mohandas Gandhi, had much better success, reaching across religious and ethnic lines with his broader appeal to Indian nationalism.

Even so, there is much at stake in Indian politics this year [2001]. The current government, led by the Hindu nationalist Bharatiya Janata Party and its coalition partners, has a razor-thin majority in parliament.

Upcoming state elections in the highly populated Uttar Pradesh—which includes Allahabad—could weaken the BJP further, especially if voters use it to voice their displeasure with the local economy. For this reason alone, it's easy to see the political appeal of these millions of devout voters.

Recently, Sonia Gandhi, the Italian-born head of India's Congress Party, took a waist-high dip and paid her respects to a few Hindu saints.

Interview with David Frawley, Vedanta Scholar and Teacher, About the Hindu Awakening

Suma Varughese: Is the Hindu nationalistic awakening good and positive?

David Frawley: I would most agree with V.S. Naipaul. Overall, every awakening has its fringe groups; for instance, when the blacks in America awakened on civil rights issues, there were extremist groups. For Hindus the awakening is necessary today. The Christians have done it, the Muslims have done it, even the Buddhists have done it. Hindus need to say that we have a place in the world, we have a point of view, you don't need to step on us. . . .

You must be aware that Indian HRD [Human Resource Development] minister, Murli Manohar Joshi, is trying to introduce a more traditional interpretation of Indian history.

It's necessary. Unfortunately, most of the history texts are written by Marxists who don't like India and Hinduism. . . . India as a country needs to claim its own educational heritage. In the USA we can study about the Puritans as part of the development of American culture. Why can't you study the Mahabharata as a participatory part of your history? All over the world there has been a movement away from the colonial interpretation of history. In America, the blacks said we want the interpretation of history from our perspective—we don't want the colonial view, the Marxist view, the missionary view. And that needs to be changed in India too.

*David Frawley, interviewed by Suma Varughese,
Life Positive, May 2002.*

More significantly, the Vishwa Hindu Parishad, the powerful Hindu nationalist group that backs the current BJP government, has used the Kumbh as a platform for drumming up support for its planned Hindu temple on the site of a mosque demolished in 1992, an act that sparked deadly riots.

By far, the most politically active at the Kumbh fairgrounds are the members of the Vishwa Hindu Parishad, a group as influential in Indian politics as the Christian Coalition is in America.

Not far from the main bathing area, under the vast yellow and saffron tent of the VHP, a group of Hindu saints, sadhus, and pilgrims discuss current events. The session wouldn't be out of place in a Delhi salon, but it is unprecedented at the Kumbh Mela.

The group makes a bevy of demands, including cleaning up the Ganges, halting the slaughter of cows, opposing Christian and Muslim conversions, and building the Ram temple at the disputed site in Ayodhya. Ram is one of the most important gods in Hindu mythology.

One aspect of Indian politics sets it apart from, say, the US House of Representatives: the presence of religion in politics. Instead of calling for a vote of yea or nay, the Hindu parliamentarians pass each proposal with a call of "Jai Shri Ram," or "Victory to Lord Ram."

Outside the tent here in Allahabad, pilgrims voice their support for this brand of Hindu politics, particularly on the Ram temple issue.

"Every Hindu is quite ready for the temple to be built," says M. Yadav of the northern city of Azamgarh. "No power can break it, no power can stop it."

R.N. Saraswatiji of New Delhi agrees, but thinks the temple should be built immediately, without waiting for a pending court case to resolve the dispute between Muslims and Hindus.

"The results should come sooner," Mr. Saraswatiji says, to the approval of a gathered throng of listeners.

Spiritual Rejuvenation

But away from this saffron-colored tent, most Hindus seem less willing to be distracted from their main goal: a cleansing dip in the muddy Ganges, and the promise of a fresh start.

Some take boats out to a sand bar at the confluence of the two rivers to avoid the crowds. There, women in saris, and men in their skivvies jump in the water and immerse themselves repeatedly while chanting a prayer.

Other folks stick to the riverbank, bathing and launching little boats of rice or flowers or small candles into the river, letting the currents take their prayers to the gods.

Physicist R.C. Tripathi of Allahabad says he has attended every Kumbh Mela since 1966.

"I'm trying to get eternal bliss of the old days," he says. "But I don't come on the main bathing days," he adds with a laugh, "because I'm not sure I'm going to survive."

Further down the bank, as one mother takes her shivering infant out of the cold water and another drags a terrified toddler in, a pilgrim from the Kashmiri city of Jammu named Bhardwaj says everyone needs a spiritual cleansing now and then.

"If you purchase a beautiful vehicle, you do all the washing and oil change and you give it gasoline, but even then it has to be sent for an overhaul," Bhardwaj says. "In this workaday world, a little overhauling is necessary."

> *"Four million Kashmiri Muslims . . . suffer every day the misery and degradation of a full-fledged military occupation."*

India's Dispute with Pakistan over Kashmir Is at a Breaking Point

Pankaj Mishra

According to Pankaj Mishra in the following viewpoint, the India-Pakistan conflict over the disputed land of Kashmir is endangering the region. India's military occupation of Kashmir, in Mishra's view, is threatening and angering its people. Moreover, by unleashing violence against peaceful protesters, India is provoking young people to turn to arms, Mishra cautions. He recommends that India allow Kashmir more freedoms. Mishra recently published the book Temptations of the West: How to Be Modern in India, Pakistan, Tibet, and Beyond *about his travels through Kashmir and other parts of Asia.*

As you read, consider the following questions:

1. How many people have been killed in the violence over Kashmir, in the author's estimation?

Pankaj Mishra, "A Jihad Grows in Kashmir," *New York Times*, August 27, 2008, p. A23.

2. What did the survey by Doctors Without Borders discover, according to Mishra?

3. What does the author suggest as the first steps India should take to help the Kashmiri people meet their aspirations for better lives?

For more than a week now, hundreds of thousands of Muslims have filled the streets of Srinagar, the capital of Indian-ruled Kashmir, shouting "azadi" (freedom) and raising the green flag of Islam. These demonstrations, the largest in nearly two decades, remind many of us why in 2000 President Bill Clinton described Kashmir, the Himalayan region claimed by both India and Pakistan, as "the most dangerous place on earth."

Mr. Clinton sounded a bit hyperbolic back then. Dangerous, you wanted to ask, to whom? Though more than a decade old, the anti-Indian insurgency in Kashmir, which Pakistan's rogue intelligence agency had infiltrated with jihadi terrorists, was not much known outside South Asia. But then the Clinton administration had found itself compelled to intervene in 1999 when India and Pakistan fought a limited but brutal war near the so-called line of control that divides Indian Kashmir from the Pakistani-held portion of the formerly independent state. Pakistan's withdrawal of its soldiers from high peaks in Indian Kashmir set off the series of destabilizing events that culminated in Pervez Musharraf assuming power in a military coup.

After 9/11, Mr. Musharraf quickly became the Bush administration's ally. Seen through the fog of the "war on terror" and the Indian government's own cynical propaganda, the problem in Kashmir seemed entirely to do with jihadist terrorists. President Musharraf could even claim credit for fighting extremism by reducing his intelligence service's commitment to jihad in Kashmir—indeed, he did help bring down the level of violence, which has claimed an estimated 80,000 lives.

Since then Pakistan has developed its own troubles with Muslim extremists. Conventional wisdom now has Pakistan down as the most dangerous place on earth. Meanwhile, India is usually tagged as a "rising superpower" or "capitalist success story"—cliches so pervasive that they persuaded even so shrewd an observer as Fareed Zakaria to claim in his new book *The Post-American World* that India since 1997 has been "stable, peaceful and prosperous."

It is true that India's relations with Pakistan have improved lately. But more than half a million Indian soldiers still pursue a few thousand insurgents in Kashmir. While periodically holding bilateral talks with Pakistan, India has taken for granted those most affected by the so-called Kashmir dispute: the four million Kashmiri Muslims who suffer every day the misery and degradation of a full-fledged military occupation.

The Indian government's insistence that peace is spreading in Kashmir is at odds with a report by Human Rights Watch in 2006 that described a steady pattern of arbitrary arrest, torture and extrajudicial execution by Indian security forces— excesses that make the events at Abu Ghraib seem like a case of high spirits. A survey by Doctors Without Borders in 2005 found that Muslim women in Kashmir, prey to the Indian troops and paramilitaries, suffered some of the most pervasive sexual violence in the world.

Over the last two decades, most ordinary Kashmiri Muslims have wavered between active insurrection and sullen rage. They fear, justifiably or not, the possibility of Israeli-style settlements by Hindus; reports two months ago of a government move to grant 92 acres of Kashmiri land to a Hindu religious group are what provoked the younger generation into the public defiance expressed of late.

As always, the turmoil in Kashmir heartens extremists in both India and Pakistan. India has recently suffered a series of terrorist bombings, allegedly by radicals among its Muslim minority. Hindu nationalists have already formed an economic blockade of the Kashmir Valley—an attempt to punish seditious Muslims and to gin up votes in next year's general elections. In Pakistan, where weak civilian governments in the past sought to score populist points by stirring up the emotional issue of Kashmir, the intelligence service can only be gratified by another opportunity to synergize its jihads in Kashmir and Afghanistan.

What of the Kashmiris themselves, who have repeatedly found themselves reduced to pawns in the geopolitical games and domestic politics of their neighbors? In 1989 and '90, when few Kashmiris had heard of Osama bin Laden, hundreds of thousands of Muslims buoyed by popular revolutions in Eastern Europe regularly petitioned the United Nations office in Srinagar, hoping to raise the world's sympathy for their cause. Indian troops responded by firing into many of these largely peaceful demonstrations, killing hundreds of people and provoking many young Kashmiris to take to arms and embrace radical Islam.

A new generation of politicized Kashmiris has now risen; the world is again likely to ignore them—until some of them turn into terrorists with al Qaeda links. It is up to the Indian government to reckon honestly with Kashmiri aspirations for a life without constant fear and humiliation. Some first steps are obvious: to severely cut the numbers of troops in Kashmir; to lift the economic blockade on the Kashmir Valley; and to allow Kashmiris to trade freely across the line of control with Pakistan.

India's record of pitiless intransigence does not inspire much hope that it will take these necessary steps toward the final and comprehensive resolution of Kashmir's long-disputed status. In fact, an indefinite curfew has already been imposed

Kashmiri Deaths and Disappearances Are Common

Since the Muslim insurgency began in Indian Kashmir 17 years ago, thousands of Kashmiris have been killed or disappeared. Kashmiris claim that many of the deaths and disappearances followed arrests by Indian security forces.

The Indian army moved thousands of troops into the region at the beginning of the 1990s, when Muslim militants, with backing from Pakistan, infiltrated Indian-Kashmir and began targeting Hindu residents. A reign of bombings, kidnappings and high-level assassinations during the early years of the insurgency drove an estimated 100,000 Hindu Kashmiris, known as "Pandits," from the valley.

Since then the Indian army has established a firm hold on the region, and the insurgency has waned, but there are still skirmishes and claims of human rights abuses by Indian forces.

Staged gun battles, called "fake encounters" by many Kashmiris, have become common practice in the disputed territory. In these encounters, Kashmiri civilians are killed by Indian security forces, which accuse them of militant behavior. Officials with the security forces say that flushing out these elements are part of legitimate counterinsurgencies operations.

By the Indian government's estimates, the number of Kashmiris missing or killed in the so-called fake encounters is just over 1,000. But human rights groups put the number at ten times that amount.

Anuj Chopra, "Kashmir: A Troubled Paradise,"
PBS Frontline/World, July 20, 2007.

and Indian troops have again killed dozens of demonstrators. But a brutal suppression of the nonviolent protests will continue to radicalize a new generation of Muslims and engender a fresh cycle of violence, rendering Kashmir even more dangerous—and not just to South Asia this time.

| *"We have to respect water and not treat it as a commodity or something to be merely consumed."*

India's Water Crisis Has Reached Critical Levels

Nitya Jacob, as told to Frederick Noronha

In the viewpoint that follows, journalist Frederick Noronha interviews Nitya Jacob, environmental expert and author of Jalyatra: Exploring India's Traditional Water Management Systems. *Jacob maintains that India is embroiled in a water crisis due to pollution and mismanagement of resources. He claims that many Indians waste water and expect an unlimited water supply. Industries overuse water as well, he adds. The management of water resources, in Jacob's contention, should be community-driven rather than delegated to the government.*

As you read, consider the following questions:

1. What are the three most surprising things the author discovered about water while researching his book?

2. What evidence does Jacob provide to show that religion and water are linked?

3. In Jacob's view, how is the soft drink and bottled water industry swaying people's opinions on water?

Former business and environmental journalist Nitya Jacob has undertaken an unusual task—an ecological travelogue across the Indian subcontinent focused on water.

The Delhi-based writer's findings are stark. After writing a book on the subject, he says that in spite of surplus water, and one of the world's richest traditions of managing it, India's water crisis has reached critical levels.

Jacob's new book is called *Jalyatra: Exploring India's Traditional Water Management Systems*. In it he observes, "The 5,000 years worth of traditional knowledge which made India one of the richest countries in the not-too-distant past has been forgotten and is one of the main reasons behind the crisis."

Frederick Noronha: How would you describe the book?

Nitya Jacob: It's an ecological travelogue that looks at links between water, society and places in an easy-to-read manner.

This book places water resources in the local environmental and social context. It does so to make the case that water management evolved in keeping with local conditions to serve local populations.

Sometimes water works were undertaken to employ people. But these were usually constructed to ensure there was enough water for agriculture and human consumption, to tide over years when rains failed. The book also brings out the cultural and religious links with water in India.

The Historical Importance of Water Is Great

Why focus on water at all?

Life began in water and we use it for everything—drinking, breathing, eating, bathing, farming, manufacturing, clothing, etc. It's one of the four life forces. But we disrespect it, and I wanted to change that.

What inspired you to take up this task, on a matter so many take for granted?

I have been writing on the environment for several years, and during my time at [India's premier environmental magazine] *Down To Earth* I got a glimpse at the diversity of water resources in India.

During this time, I was in touch with several people working on water who are mentioned in the book, including Rajender Singh and Ramesh Pahadi.

From them, I heard about the centuries-old water structures and the way people used to revere water and use it carefully.

This diversity prompted me to suggest the idea to my friend Karthika in Penguin, who told me to write a book. Once I started, it was a fascinating journey from water to water.

It was hard to decide which states to select, as each has very different traditions.

What were the three most surprising finds from the book?

Firstly, the sheer diversity of water wisdom as reflected in the types of water management structures. Secondly, the depth of knowledge that the ancients had about constructing water structures. Thirdly, the extent to which water was respected as the giver and destroyer of life are the three most surprising finds from the book.

The Water-Religion Connection

What do you see as the major lessons that emerge?

We have to respect water and not treat it as a commodity or something to be merely consumed. We have done this for too long, and our thinking has been shaped by a Westernized education system. Those 'ignorant peasants' know more about this than most engineers today.

With respect comes the desire to use water wisely, to conserve it and protect its sources. This becomes an almost religious pursuit.

There is ample evidence to show that religion and water are interlinked. Each temple has a source of water, each mosque has a pond for washing, each gurudwara has a pond, and churches have the baptism fonts. No place of worship is complete without a source of water.

India's diverse eco-agro-climatic-social zones have evolved their own systems, that if restored, can meet a large part of the need of people for drinking water and farming. We have to carry the past along, not bury it in dams and canals. There is a meeting point, that requires thinking through and dialogue.

By the same argument, water resources management has to become localized and community-driven. Large centralized construction and maintenance systems cannot work in the long run because they are costly, inequitable, do not involve local people and are always seen as exploitative, which is why most pipes leak.

Water management is as much a social-cultural issue as it is an environmental and technical one. But this has always been ignored in modern solutions. As far as possible, social structures and mechanisms that governed water resource use have to be mapped onto modern technical solutions and technology that does not fit social needs has to go.

For too long we have tried the reverse approach; it's time to change that.

Society has become lazy and adopted the government-will-provide attitude. If the water supply is disrupted, or canals do not have water at a particular time, people blame the government.

I have found the willingness to take the initiative and help ourselves within the law is lacking. Civil society cannot expect the government to provide because what it provides is waste

The Death of the Holy Yamuna River

The fabled Yamuna River, on whose banks [New Delhi] was born more than 2,000 years ago, is a case study in the water management crisis confronting India.

In Hindu mythology, the Yamuna is considered to be a river that fell from heaven to earth. Today, it is a foul portrait of crippled infrastructure—and yet, still worshiped. From the bridges that soar across the river, the faithful toss coins and sweets, lovingly wrapped in plastic. They scatter the ashes of their dead.

In New Delhi the Yamuna itself is clinically dead.

As the Yamuna enters the capital, still relatively clean from its 246-mile descent from atop the Himalayas, the city's public water agency, the New Delhi Jal Board, extracts 229 million gallons every day from the river, its largest single source of drinking water.

As the Yamuna leaves the city, it becomes the principal drain for New Delhi's waste. Residents pour 950 million gallons of sewage into the river each day.

Somini Sengupta, New York Times, *September 29, 2006.*

and misused. The government has a new-found willingness, at nearly all levels, to engage with people and the public has to push the envelope.

Water Greed

How would you describe the water situation in India today?

We are in a crisis of our own making but things haven't gone out of control yet. We have plenty of water, but people have abdicated their role in looking after these resources to the government.

Part of the problem has to do with supply—the only solution the government has is large projects because the lure of lucre. The other part is demand, and we expect 24x7 supplies of water without lifting a finger. And we also waste water when we have it.

Farmers over-irrigate because nobody has told them how much water is really needed to optimize food production. None of the farmers I spoke to had any idea how much water is actually needed because all farm extension workers or seed and fertilizer sellers tell them is the amount of fertilizer and pesticides needed, not water.

In cities that suck up water resources from miles around, supply pipes leak or are tapped by the poor, while the rich water lawns and dig ever-deeper tubewells. They put pumps on the water mains to suck out water.

We are greedy and driven by the shortage mindset, when actually we need to watch what we are using. Industrial use is masked because they depend heavily on tankers and groundwater, both of which are tough to monitor. But industry believes the show must go on and therefore sources water regardless of quality or cost.

Then we have the burgeoning water and soft drinks industry. I must have travelled 10,000 kilometers (6,000 miles) and visited hundreds of villages, and always drank water that was available there, sourced from wells, handpumps, streams, tanks and tubewells.

I didn't fall sick. The soft drinks/bottled water industry would have us believe we have poison coming out of our taps that also tastes bad, and therefore we must buy their water. That is utter bullshit.

Low cost purification—filtration or boiling—is more than enough to safeguard our health at home and while traveling. Almost all towns have the candle-water filters.

In any case, there have been plenty of tests on bottled water that have shown they are as contaminated with bacteria as regular tap water that has been filtered. The crisis then is of perceptions, supply and demand. But we haven't reached the tipping point yet.

A Personal Interest in Water

Tell us something about your own past connections with water.

As a child, I enjoyed tub baths but felt a pang of guilt at the hundreds of liters of water I wasted in every bath. I've enjoyed the seaside whenever I have had the luxury of visiting it.

As a child I would cup my hands over my ears and pretend to listen to the sound of the sea, like a voice in the sky. When I started journalism as a sub-editor/reporter in a business paper, I used to pay particular attention to water.

In 1990, Intach [Indian National Trust for Art and Cultural Heritage] launched a campaign against the Tehri Dam [in Uttaranchal], and I visited the site. The appalling destruction overshadowed everything else—it was a moonscape where the river flowed and the hills were denuded.

That was the first practical wake up call I got and later, in *Down To Earth*, and since then I have followed water-related subjects with particular interest. I have known Rajender Singh since 1992 and have followed his work closely as well.

In 1992, I toured the entire Narmada valley that's now under water. I wrote on that for *Down To Earth* [an Indian environmental magazine].

Since then, off and on I have written on water and [since 2005] have been closely involved with it. I am now the resource person for the Water Community of Solution Exchange that discusses issues related to water—governance, water resources management, drinking water, sanitation and water use in agriculture.

Conservation Initiatives

Which states, in your view, are doing the most interesting work on water in India today?

If you refer to the governments, Tamil Nadu has initiated a lot of work on rainwater harvesting and tank regeneration. If you rate it in terms of people's initiatives, there have been very successful attempts to revive water harvesting in both Gujarat and Rajasthan, because of the severe shortage of drinking water, fluoride contamination and salinity in groundwater.

The interesting part of these initiatives is community involvement where community management structures have been successfully mapped onto the revival program.

What are the biggest challenges on the water front that India currently faces in your view?

Mismanagement of water resources, pollution from natural and manmade sources, and increasing disparities in availability due to changing rainfall, and shrinking surface storage and rivers being tapped at various points.

Periodical Bibliography

The following articles have been selected to supplement the diverse views presented in this chapter.

Matthew Connelly   "Population Control in India: Prologue to the Emergency Period," *Population and Development Review*, December 2006.

Sarah Crowe   "Food Crisis Ravages India's Poorest Children," UNICEF, June 9, 2008.

Abhijit Das   "The Ethical Implications of the Targeted Population Programme Proposed by the PA," *Indian Journal of Medical Ethics*, January–March 2005.

R.C. Lahoti, as told to Sreelatha Menon   "'A Judgment Can't Be a Solution to All the Problems,'" *Times of India*, March 21, 2006.

Ashish Mehta   "India to Face Severe Water Crisis by 2045: Expert," Indo-Asian News Service, March 28, 2007.

Kuldip Nayar   "Gujarat Poses Challenge to Indian Secularism," *Gulf News* (Dubai), June 28, 2008.

Abhik Roy   "Regenerating Masculinity in the Construction of Hindu Nationalist Identity: A Case Study of Shiv Sena," *Communication Studies*, June 2006.

Mohit Sahni et al.   "Missing Girls in India: Infanticide, Feticide and Made-to-Order Pregnancies?" *PLoS One*, May 21, 2008.

Somini Sengupta   "In Teeming India, Water Crisis Means Dry Pipes and Foul Sludge," *New York Times*, September 29, 2006.

OPPOSING
VIEWPOINTS®
SERIES

CHAPTER 3

What Is the Status of Human Rights in India?

Chapter Preface

India, from its decrepit slums to the Taj Mahal, is a land of contradictions. "India presents a paradox," observes Mani Bhaumik—himself a study in contrasts, as he is a highly spiritual physicist. "It is profound and primitive, deeply spiritual and darkly superstitious, both universalistic and maddeningly provincial." Such incongruity is equally apparent in the treatment of women. Oppressed in some ways but liberated in others, Indian women sometimes find themselves restricted by the laws and processes meant to uplift them. For example, the country recently granted women the right to inherit property when their fathers die, yet fathers can repeal that right. Dowry, originally given to a bride as a wedding gift and as security in case she is mistreated, is now illegal because it came to be used as a bribe paid to the husband's family that thousands of women are harassed or killed over. All of these conflicts hint that agreement over women's rights, and how to safeguard them, is difficult to reach.

Under British rule, females in India were seen as weaker and less important than their male counterparts. Since then, women have made inroads in reaching equality. In 1993, for instance, India amended its constitution to reserve seats for women in local government. This led to the groundbreaking elections of a million rural women and thousands of urban women to government posts, where they can shape policies important to women. Gains were seen with the election of India's first female prime minister, Indira Gandhi, in 1966 and first woman president, Pratibha Patil, in 2007. These elections proved that the candidate's skills, not his or her gender, were most important to voters and that women were up to the task of leading the country. In contrast, the United States, also a democratic country, still awaits its first female commander. Indian women are employed in other traditionally male-only sectors, and they enjoy many of the same rights and activities as do men.

Despite these gains, women continue to face special challenges unique to India. Boys are openly preferred to girls in much of the country. Such inequality is reinforced by the caste system, conservative sex roles, and certain religious customs in India. Younger members of some families have shunned arranged marriages and insist on choosing a spouse they love. It follows that more unions based on love means more separations for those who fall out of love. Columnist Anand Giridharadas asserts,

> Ever more couples marry each other for each other, out of personal enthrallment rather than a sense of family duty, and even arranged marriages come with new expectations of emotional fulfillment. And it is this new notion of love, with the couple at the core, that makes marriage both more riveting and more precarious than ever before.

An uptick in divorces also speaks to women's independence and empowerment, according to feminists. With more women in the workplace and less dependent on their husbands, wives can afford to leave an unhappy marriage. Ranjana Kumari, author of *Brides Are Not for Burning*, avers, "In the past, women had little or no choice but to stay with their husbands except in instances of extreme abuse or cruelty. . . . With economic empowerment, that is no longer so."

The overall significance of rising divorce rates in India remains to be seen. The factors affecting change in the country is a subject of contention in the following chapter, in which authors set forth predictions and goals for the coming years.

> "This law ... not only discriminates based on gender (man vs. woman), but also discriminates against women based on their relationship with the husband."

The Dowry and Cruelty Law Harms Men and Their Families

Asha-Kiran

In the following viewpoint, the men's legal rights organization Asha-Kiran charges that a dowry and cruelty law meant to protect women threatens innocent husbands and breaks up families. The group contends that those accused of harassing their wives or female in-laws are arrested under the law without evidence and that some have been driven to suicide. Few of these accusations, from the organization's point of view, are legitimate. The law, according to Asha-Kiran, is discriminatory, since it allows no men and only certain women to file complaints. Asha-Kiran seeks to correct laws and stereotypes that discriminate towards men.

Asha-Kiran, *Indian Dowry Law (498A): Myth vs. Reality*. Bangalore, INDIA: Asha-Kiran, 2006. Copyright © 2006 RAKSHAK FOUNDATION. Reproduced by permission.

As you read, consider the following questions:

1. How many people are affected by false accusations under 498a, in Asha-Kiran's estimation?

2. In what way does the provision lead to cruelty towards children, according to the author?

3. What does the author of *Harassed Husband* warn will happen if misuse of 498a continues, according to Asha-Kiran?

There is a rapidly escalating social evil in Indian families, namely the misuse of the Dowry and Cruelty laws (Criminal Laws), which were originally meant to act "as a shield" for the protection of harassed women. Nowadays, the educated urban Indian women have turned the tables. They have discovered several loopholes in the existing Indian judicial system and are using the dowry laws to harass all or most of the husband's family that includes mothers, sisters, sisters-in-law, elderly grandparents, disabled individuals and even very young children.

We are not talking about the dowry deaths or physical injury cases but about dowry harassment cases that require no evidence and can be filed just based on a single-sentence complaint by the wife. With an approximately 65,000 such accusations per year, about 200,000 people are directly affected by these false accusations. The number of such cases has increased by about 100% in the last 10 years and by more than 15% in just the last two years. This poorly formulated law is inviting unscrupulous people to file false cases, and causing the imprisonment of innocent people without investigation. These innocent people undergo stigmatization and hardship even before a trial in the court of law which leads to immense emotional, physical and financial trauma. Unable to bear the harassment, the loss of reputation and the social consequences of being implicated in a false criminal case, some of these falsely accused husbands and their elderly parents are committing suicide.

Despite the recommendations of the Supreme Court of India and Justice Malimath Committee that the legislative arm should modify the laws such that the innocent are protected, the suggested amendments to the law have been largely ignored. Unconstrained, this social evil is threatening the foundation of the Indian Family system.

We are a large group of several thousand families unwilling to succumb to Legal Terrorism, with a belief that *truth shall prevail.*

What Is Section 498a of the IPC (Indian Penal Code)?

Section 498a of the IPC is a criminal law in which the wife and her family can charge any or all of the husband's family of physical or mental cruelty. This law is unique to India as it not only discriminates based on gender (man vs. woman), but also discriminates against women based on their relationship with the husband. Typically, the charged family members in these cases include:

- Mostly women of all ages (unmarried, married and pregnant sisters of the husband, his mother and sisters-in-law, elderly grandmothers and aunts)

- Other maternal and paternal relatives and even young children in the family

For every complaint filed by a woman, there are generally twice as many or more women are accused although the married couple may have never lived with any of the people mentioned in the criminal complaint

IPC-498a is

- Cognizable—The accused can be arrested and jailed without warrant or investigation

- Non-Compoundable—The complaint cannot be withdrawn by the petitioner

- Non-Bailable—The accused must appear in the court to request bail

The accused are presumed guilty, and for all practical purposes, the burden is on the accused to prove innocence in the courts. The FIR is typically an imaginary story, running into many pages, with absolutely no supporting evidence. It typically takes about 7 to 8 years for the accused to prove their innocence in the courts. Due to the overwhelmingly large number of false cases, the conviction rate in these cases is close to zero. The delay in the provision of justice amounts to the denial of justice.

There is no penalty for the misuse of IPC 498a, and after acquittal of the accused, the courts are reluctant to entertain defamation and perjury cases against the falsely testifying witnesses.

Why do people misuse IPC 498a?

- Legal Extortion—Get-rich-quick-scheme to extort large amounts of money

- Prior Relationship—Wife has a prior relationship, and cannot get out of it. She marries to satisfy her parents, and then misuses the 498a law in order to obtain a divorce

- Adultery—Women who indulge in adultery use 498a as a bargaining tool

- Domination—Wife wants the husband to abandon his parents and siblings, and have total control over his finances and social behavior

Many Speak Out Against the Dowry Law

Please take a moment to read through what a lot of newspapers, judiciary and media are saying about IPC-498a (commonly known as Indian dowry law).

"Nowadays lots of men are experiencing pre-wedding jitters. The reason: They are terrified of misuse of the anti-dowry law."—*Vijay Times*, Bangalore, Thursday 07 April, 2005

"The police should realize that it is not a matter between two individuals, not even between two families, but several families, such as in-laws"—*The Hindu*, September 17th, 2004

"It's time that the law is changed and punishment for these false accusations be made the same as that meted out to those who are really guilty of such acts." "The anti dowry law has a number of loopholes and it is high time that our society wakes up and takes a strong note to amend these one-sided laws which are eventually breaking up our Indian marriage system" —www.hindustan.net, July 27th, 2005

Asha-Kiran,
Indian Dowry Law (498a):
Myth vs. Reality, *April 2006.*

- Custody—Deny the father and his family access to their child(ren).

- Fraudulent Marriages—in which the bride (and her family) hides her education level or mental health; and when is justifiably asked to release the person who has gone into marriage without knowing the full facts; she files a false 498a case.

What Do the Courts, Governments and Non-Government Organizations (NGO) Say?

- The Supreme Court and High Courts have acknowledged this 'misuse' as a growing menace in the society and have recommended the legislature to amend the law

- Justice Malimath committee recommended that IPC 498a be made bailable and compoundable

- The US State Department has issued a travel warning regarding the misuse of dowry laws in India, and highlighted the fact that Indian courts require large sums of money to settle such cases

- The Canadian Government has issued a similar warning

- The WHO has explicitly mentioned that 498A is one of biggest reasons for elder abuse in India

- Many women's organizations, including several State Commissions for Women, have acknowledged the misuse of these laws and have recommended similar protection for men

What Does 498a do to Society?

- Abuse of the Criminal Judicial System

- Elder Abuse—Most senior citizens who have never been to the police stations or courts in their lifetime are dragged into jail without investigation and then into court cases that span several years

- Women Abuse—Many women in the husband's family are abused by the process

- Abuse of entire extended family—Many in the husband's family lose their jobs/earnings

- Cruelty towards Children—Separation of parents from children, including infants results in trauma

- Unequal rights (not only women vs. men but also women vs. women)—The wife/daughter-in-law can file charges against all the women in the husband's family even if they are innocent but the female relatives of a husband do not have similar legal provisions for protection from a daughter-in-law or sister-in-law even in cases where she is abusive

- Disintegration of families—Due to fear of being implicated in a false 498A case, parents have now started to legally disown their sons before or immediately after marriage. The terror of this law has resulted in the break up of numerous families

- Suicides of innocent people—Unable to bear the harassment and the humiliation they suffer after being charged in a false criminal case, many people, including aged senior citizens, have been committing suicides

The number of innocent families victimized by the misuse of 498a is increasing alarmingly. These innocent families are looked upon as culprits by the neighbors, the society and the law enforcement authorities when police visit their home and arrest them. Some of them, have committed suicide because of the ignominy they had to suffer. "There have been instances where mother or father have died of shock or committed suicide because the humiliation of a false criminal case was too much to bear," writes Kusum, a prolific writer on gender issue, in her thought provoking book "Harassed Husband". "If this trend continues it is not unlikely that women themselves might suffer as they would lose credibility and sympathy of the society. Innocent, simple girls are more likely to suffer because of malicious complaints by clever and unscrupulous women", Kusum warns. Many men have also committed suicide rather than face humiliation.

A bank employee hanged himself in his flat in Maya Puri, Delhi. The wife often used to stay with her parents. His efforts to persuade his wife to return to his home only resulted in his wife filing a false dowry complaint against him. Another man immolated himself in New Delhi. The reason being complaint of 'dowry demand' by his estranged wife which led him to jail twice. A 40-year-old ex-Airforce officer, committed suicide in Ahmedabad, Gujarat, after being implicated in a false 498A case during which he was jailed for 10 days. Unable to cope with the "mental torture" inflicted by his wife, a 30-year-old man committed suicide in Krishnagar, West Bengal, on Jan 3, 2007. He had been dragged to the police station, on at least a dozen occasions in the past five years, by his wife, complaining of torture, which were confirmed to be false by the additional superintendent of police. Another man committed suicide in Ahmedabad on Nov 19, 2006 after being harassed in a false 498A case. He was the only son of his aged parents. A 30-year-old man from Kolkata committed suicide on Sept 1, 2006, after being implicated and arrested in a 498A case in 1999. Even after 7 years, his case was subjudice when he died.

Numerous senior citizens are also committing suicide due to harassment faced due to false 498A cases. A 64-year-old man, a retired employee of a multi-national company, committed suicide in Kolkata, explicitly mentioning about 498A in his suicide note stating further that "I am ending my life unable to bear the torture meted out to me by my daughter-in-law". Another senior citizen from Ludhiana, Punjab, killed himself by throwing himself before a running train and left behind a suicide note that read "I am ending my life because the parents-in-law of my son have filed false cases against me and my family".

An old couple from Faridkot, Punjab, killed themselves by consuming pesticides on Jun 20, 2006. It was revealed that the deceased were feeling harassed and terrorized after their daughter-in-law got a criminal case registered against them for bringing insufficient dowry. Humiliated and on the run, they committed suicide clarifying in the suicide note that they never harassed their daughter-in-law for dowry.

The terror of this law has completely destroyed and annihilated several innocent families. An entire family consumed poison on Feb 3, 2007 in Alwar, Rajasthan. The husband, an engineer, and his father died, while his mother was admitted to hospital. Right from the starting of marriage, the bride's family used to harass the husband by threatening to implicate him and his entire family in the false cases related to Dowry. Another instance of mass suicide involving three members of a family was reported a few years ago in Ballabgarh, Haryana. In this case, the husband himself, his young sister and their hapless mother consumed poison and ended their lives because of the growing unreasonable demand of the daughter-in-law and the continuous harassment inflicted by her family.

These few instances illustrate the terror that has been created by anti-dowry laws in the minds of a large number of husbands who feel captive in the hands of their own wives. While some hapless men, unable to live a harassed and humiliated married life, prefer to die, many others live their married lives under constant fear of being falsely implicated under section 498a. They are forced to meet unreasonable demands, tolerating unruly behavior of their wives only for family's *Izzat*.

For more information on human rights, please visit these Web sites:

- http://documents.rakshakfoundation.org
- http://data.rakshakfoundation.org

- http://www.rakshakfoundation.org/links/498aMisuse.pdf
- http://www.rakshakfoundation.org/links/ReportFor Parliament.pdf

"The provision had been brought in because the increase in the number of dowry deaths was a matter of serious concern."

The Dowry and Cruelty Law Protects Women and Is Constitutional

Rakesh Shukla

In the following viewpoint, Rakesh Shukla, a Supreme Court lawyer in India, explains that the dowry and cruelty provision protects women from harassment by their husbands and his relatives. Giving, taking, or demanding dowry—payment from a bride's family to her husband's—is already forbidden, Shukla contends. However, dowry harassment legislation has been hindered in the past and in his opinion, punishments must be made certain in order to deter dowry demands. Though the author concedes there may be difficulty in eliminating dowry acceptance, he emphasizes that the dowry harassment law is constitutional and necessary.

As you read, consider the following questions:

1. What are four reasons the law's opponents cite for women who implicate their husbands under Section 498-A, in the author's contention?

2. According to Justice Balasubramanyan in the viewpoint, how was dowry seen in earlier times?

3. Name three things the Supreme Court directed the Union government and the states to do in the implementation of the Dowry Prohibition Act.

Given the widespread violence and cruelty inflicted upon women, Section 498-A, dealing with cruelty towards a woman by her husband or his relatives, was introduced in the Indian Penal Code (IPC) through an amendment in 1983. What led to the enactment of this provision was the realisation that cruelty against a woman by her husband or his relatives, culminating in murder or suicide, constituted only a small fraction of cases involving cruelty against women.

For the first time, the section made it punishable (three years' imprisonment and a fine) for a husband or his relatives to subject a woman to cruelty. The law explicitly recognised mental cruelty and mental health. Cruelty was defined as any conduct likely to cause grave injury or danger to life, limb, the mental or physical health of a woman, or to drive her to commit suicide. Harassment or coercion of a woman or her relatives to fulfill demands for money or property was included within the definition of 'cruelty'.

Attacks on the Provision

Since its enactment, this provision has been subject to systematic and sustained attack. It has been called unfair and responsible for the victimisation of husbands by their wives and her relatives. A sizeable section of society holds this view and articulates it through articles in newspapers and magazines.

"To get a share of the property," "vengeance," "blackmail," "to teach a lesson," are some of the reasons cited for women wanting to implicate their husbands under this law.

The constitutionality of Section 498-A has also been challenged in court. Sushil Kumar Sharma, in a petition before the apex court, asked that the provision be struck down, or alternative guidelines be formulated so that the innocent are not victimised by unscrupulous persons making false accusations. According to Sharma, there was no "prosecution" in these cases, only "persecution". Several instances were cited to show that allegations of offences being committed under the provision were made with oblique motives and with a view to harassing the husband, in-laws and relatives. The petitioner sought strict action against the complainants if the allegations are proved to be unfounded, in order to discourage people from approaching the courts with "unclean hands and ulterior motives". It was submitted that people tried to take undue advantage of the sympathies exhibited by the courts in matters related to alleged dowry torture, and that the accusers were (often) more at fault than the accused. Reliance was also sought on a Delhi High Court decision where concern had been expressed at the increase in the number of false and frivolous allegations.

Section 498-A Is Constitutional

The Supreme Court, in its July 19, 2005 judgment, refused to strike down the section as unconstitutional and invalid. It observed that the provision had been brought in because the increase in the number of dowry deaths was a matter of serious concern. The sphere of operation of Section 304B of the IPC, dealing with death by burns, bodily injury or any other unnatural manner of a woman being subjected to cruelty or harassment for dowry within seven years of marriage, was held to be distinct from the area covered by Section 498-A. This section was brought in specifically to deal with cases not only of dowry deaths but also of cruelty towards married women by their husbands, in-laws and relatives. It therefore made cruelty *per-se* punishable. The court also drew a distinction between Section 306 of the IPC dealing with 'abetment to suicide' and Section 498-A, holding that in the latter the woman was driven to suicide by the cruelty committed by her husband or/and his relatives, while the former dealt with an individual intending suicide abetted by another person.

Addressing the issue of abuse of the section, the court held that the mere possibility of abuse of a provision of law does not invalidate the law. In cases of abuse, it is the "action" and not the "section" that may be vulnerable. The court, while upholding the provision of law, may still set aside the action, order or decision and grant relief to the aggrieved person. The judgment quoted with approval a 1977 decision: "The wisdom of man has not yet been able conceive of government with sufficient power to answer all its legitimate needs and at the same time incapable of mischief." The court declared that if a statutory provision were otherwise intra-vires [within the legal power of congress to enact], constitutional and valid, the mere possibility of abuse of power in cases would not make it objectionable, ultra-vires [outside the bounds of congress's power] or unconstitutional.

The Creation and Amendments to the Dowry Prohibition Act

In sharp contrast to the earlier case representing the view of a section of society that believes dowry-related laws are unfair to men and are being grossly misused, the apex court recently considered a petition pointing out the failure of anti-dowry laws and pleading for effective implementation. The case is appropriately titled *In Re: Enforcement and Implementation of Dowry Prohibition Act, 1961.*

The practice of dowry was sought to be tackled by the conferment of improved property rights on women by the

The Importance of the Dowry Law

What gives [Section 498A, the "dowry law"] teeth and a terrible bite is that any offence under it is non-bailable and non-compoundable, which means it cannot be privately resolved between the parties concerned. It's also cognizable, which means it allows police to arrest the accused without investigation or warrants if a woman or close relative alleges cruelty in the marital home.

The Times of India, *"Should Dowry Law Be Diluted? The Gender War Carries On,"* September 28, 2008.

Hindu Succession Act, 1956. In addition it was felt necessary to have a law that made dowry punishable, in order to eradicate the practice. The Dowry Prohibition Act thus came to be enacted in 1961. The act made the giving and taking of dowry, as well as the demanding of dowry, an offence. However, the legislation failed to act as a check; indeed, the practice of dowry assumed ever-increasing proportions.

The matter came to be referred to a joint committee of parliament which, in 1984, resulted in certain amendments to the definition of dowry, reduced the period for return of property to the woman, and made punishments more stringent. The recommendation to take the giving of dowry out of the acts made punishable was not implemented by the government. Criminology being a little-practised science in the country, the simplistic logic of enhancing punishment to check offences prevailed yet again and the 1986 amendment to the anti-dowry act saw a further increase in the quantum of punishment for the offence. Provision for the appointment of dowry prohibition officers was also made.

The petition before the court asked for the appointment of dowry prohibition officers, directions for their functions and the establishment of advisory boards comprising social workers, as visualised under Section 8-A of the anti-dowry law. In addition, directions to central and state governments to frame rules to carry out the purposes of the act were sought.

The judgment by Justice Balasubramanyan observes that dowry may have been conceived as a nest-egg or security for the wife in her matrimonial home in earlier times, but it had now degenerated into a subject for barter, acceptance of the woman as wife depending on what her parents would pay as dowry, varying with the qualification and status of the bridegroom's family. It quotes with approval a 1946 judgment that "the high standards of the scriptural marriage which was a sacrament came to be contaminated by sordid considerations of immediate monetary gains at the sacrifice of the abiding purposes of the marriage union," and notes that the position with regard to dowry has not improved since then.

The court observed that tardy implementation of the anti-dowry law was reflected in the filing of the petition in 1997. It observed that given the fact that rules had still not been framed although the case had been pending for seven years, meant that assurances by the central and state governments with regard to effective implementation of the law could not be taken at face value.

Proper Implementation of the Anti-Dowry Law

The judgment directed the Union government and the states to effectively implement the Dowry Prohibition Act, particularly provisions dealing with the demanding and taking and giving of dowry. As part of the implementation, governments were ordered to activate the dowry prohibition officers. The Union government was directed to frame rules to make the anti-dowry law effective, and the state and Union governments directed to consider framing rules compelling males seeking government employment to furnish information on whether they had taken dowry, and if so, whether it was handed over to the wife. Similar information was to be got from those already in employment. Directions to step up anti-dowry literacy among people, through lok adalats [public grievances], radio broadcasts, television and newspapers, were also given. Governments were directed to come up with the means to create an honest, efficient and committed machinery to properly implement the Dowry Prohibition Act.

However, prospects for the implementation even of concrete steps like declaring the dowry details of government employees and prospective candidates for government jobs appear bleak. Pious declarations apart, dowry enjoys acceptance among the very officials and elected representatives responsible for its abolition. If anything, the practice of dowry has flourished over the years, smoothly enmeshed with consumerism. Its tentacles have spread even to communities that previously did not indulge in the practice.

Putting the giving of dowry on par with the taking of dowry, and making it an offence punishable with a minimum of five years' imprisonment, acts as an obstacle to cases under legislation. It victimizes the victim. As a first step, the giving of dowry should immediately be taken out of the ambit of the offence. Enhanced punishments through amendments in 1984 and 1986 have not served the purpose of checking dowry. It is not the severity of punishment but its certainty that deters people from committing an offence. The Hindu Succession (Amendment) Bill, recently passed by the Rajya Sabha, that proposes to remove discrimination against women and give daughters equal parental property rights to those of sons, is a step in the right direction. However, it may well result in daughters 'voluntarily' giving up their property rights in favour of their brothers. Perhaps we need to consider provisions to check this.

The relationship between social norms and the law is a complex one. The law can play an important but necessarily limited role in changing social norms. In the words of Jawaharlal Nehru: "Legislation cannot by itself normally solve deep-rooted social problems. One has to approach them in other ways too. But legislation is necessary and essential so that it may give that push and have that educative factor as well as the legal sanctions behind it which help public opinion to be given a certain shape."

> *"We in the Left support reservations . . . because they provide a minimum solace to the deprived sections of our society."*

Caste-Based Reservations Help Promote Equality

R. Arun Kumar

Reservation is a form of affirmative action in which a percentage of school admissions and jobs are reserved for members of India's lower castes. In the following viewpoint, R. Arun Kumar laments that children and adults of the disadvantaged classes face discrimination daily. Reservations, though imperfect, he claims, are a necessary part of ensuring equality. Kumar counters his opponents' arguments that reservations benefit the well-to-do rather than the disadvantaged. Kumar, who is president of Students' Federation of India, wrote this viewpoint for People's Democracy, *a publication of the Communist Party of India (Marxist).*

R. Arun Kumar, "Equality with Social Justice," *People's Democracy*, July 2, 2006. Reproduced by permission.

As you read, consider the following questions:

1. What are four ways in which teachers' preconceptions and biases discriminate against children from low castes, in Kumar's contention?

2. According to the Supreme Court in the Indra Sawhney case cited by the author, to what does social backwardness lead?

3. Name a social and an educational indicator of social backwardness formulated by the Mandal Commission.

"You do not take a person who, for years, has been hobbled by chains, bring him to the starting line in a race and then say, 'you are free to compete with all others'. It is not enough just to open the gates of opportunity. All our citizens must have the ability to walk through those gates"

—*[U.S. president] Lyndon Johnson (in a famous speech in 1965 that laid the foundations for the Affirmative Action.)* . . .

[In India,] discrimination based on caste is a reality. The bias on the basis of caste has a huge influence on our society with its pangs not leaving even the education system. It starts from the entry level and shadows you till you leave it. A position paper by the NCERT [National Council of Educational Research and Training], 'National Focus Group on Problems Of Scheduled Caste And Scheduled Tribe[1] Children, notes that "several studies have affirmed that educational inequality (of access and achievement) has multiple bases in the contemporary structures of caste, class, gender and ethnicity evolving in interaction with political economy". It asserts that "poverty and caste act as fundamental deterrents to education".

1. Members of a Scheduled Caste (SC) or Scheduled Tribe (ST) are in the lowest caste and were previously called untouchables. Some SCs are called Dalits and some STs are known as Adivasis.

The Reality of Caste Discrimination

Dealing extensively on the subject, [the paper] focuses on myriad ways in which caste plays a role in affecting and shaping the lives of the children. The paper notes that the physical positioning of the school too is based on caste lines. "School provisioning in predominantly scheduled caste habitations is much less as compared to general rural Habitations. . . . On the whole, higher caste habitations within larger villages are better provided". Thus at the entry level itself the children from these sections confront the problem of discrimination. The problems for the eager students from the SC families compound if they intend to study in the schools located in the upper caste villages or at least in multi-caste villages and the paper notes "hierarchical norms still govern social relations". This means that SC/ST children are simply not welcome to these schools in many villages in our country even today. The incident where a girl from Orissa was to be provided with police protection for going to a school on a bicycle is still fresh in our memory.

The paper also states the condition of the schools that exist in the SC and ST locations and the role of the teachers who are the sculptors shaping the destiny of our country in the classrooms. It states that the "teacher's social background (caste, religion, language) affect their interactions with the students". Middle class, higher caste teachers are very unhappy with the environments of schools for the poor and are poorly motivated to teach children of the poor, particularly of SC/ST background, who are derogatorily categorised as 'uneducable'. An appalling body of evidence exists which suggests that teacher's preconceptions, bias and behaviour, subtle or overt, conscious or unconscious, operate to discriminate against children of SC/ST background. Teachers are observed to have low expectations of SC/ST children and girls and generally have a condescending and downright abusive attitude to poor children from slums. Levels of hostility and indifference to dalit/tribal cultural traits and value systems are high. They "perceive dalit and adivasi children in a negative light, see them as unclean, dishonest, lazy, ill-mannered etc. The children could be criticised for their clothes, the dialect they speak, the abhorment of uncouth habits of meat eating, the ignorance of their parents and even the colour of their skin! They are punished and shouted at in efforts to discipline and 'civilise' them." The paper points out several examples to substantiate these findings: "Children are assigned a range of menial tasks—from cleaning and sweeping the school to fetching 'paan' and cigarettes for the teacher. They assign SC/ST children menial jobs and shift the onus of low learning on children and their families." The curriculum also upholds symbols of the traditional, male dominated feudal society and its obsolete cultural values and norms. The necessity for these arguments arose because the movement that has started against the intended reservations for OBCs [Other Backward Classes] has taken a position that reservations are against equality.

The Case for OBC's Reservation

It is a fact that the OBCs do not suffer to the extent as the SCs. But we should not forget the fact that the present day OBCs are the [low caste] shudras of yesteryears and they too were down the social ladder in our hierarchical caste system. This made the Supreme Court observe in the Indra Sawhney case "Social backwardness—it may be reiterated—leads to educational and economic backwardness." Majority of the OBCs are artisans. In spite of the changing generations, many occupations even to this day are 'reserved' for particular castes only. This is true in the case of fishermen, washermen, potters, barbers, weavers, stone cutters, shepherds and many of their like. Some sections among them have secured possession of land and are well off and this should not confuse us with the vast multitudes who are still poor. Whatever occupational mobility has taken place is very limited. The socio-economic 'progress' of our country ensured that the majority of the artisans did not go up the graph but took the downward trajectory. Thus we do find that many of them are living in conditions of utter deprivation and some are even forced to commit suicides. The once famed weavers of our country are next only to the peasants in the number of suicides that we have seen in the recent days because of the deteriorating economic conditions. It is but natural for the economic factors to add to the social factors and impede their educational ambitions. It is after struggling against all such heavily placed odds few from these sections are coming to higher education. It is the duty of any liberal and democratic society to provide helping hand to these sections of the society.

This reality and naked truth is unfortunately not known to those students who are protesting against reservations. The socio-economic conditions in which they are brought up and the education system did not acquaint them with these facts. Neither do the corporate 'sponsors' for their protest want them to know these facts.

The arguments that the reservations intended for these sections will be eaten away by the well-to-do sections should not be made with the intention of denying the benefits even to the needy amongst them. It is also necessary here to understand what criteria the Second Backward Classes (Mandal) Commission has adopted to determine the OBCs. The Commission worked out 11 indicators to determine social backwardness. These indicators are social, educational and economic, and as the major controversy resolves around the caste criteria allegedly adopted by the commission, it would be relevant to reproduce the actual criteria used by the Commission. The 11 indicators formulated by the commission are:

Social

- Castes/classes considered as socially backward by others.

- Castes/classes which mainly depend on manual labour for their livelihood.

Without Reservations, Discrimination Will Persist

One of the problems of the current system of reservation in the public sector is that there has been no institutional mechanism of incentives and disincentives to ensure effective affirmative action. At the moment, there are "legal" requirements for filling certain quotas, but there are no penalties for public institutions that do not fill them, or rewards for those that more than fulfill them. That is at least part of the reason why so many quotas remain unfulfilled. So this may be one of the issues that deserve greater attention: how to ensure that quotas do actually get filled.

The basic issue, of course, is that the roots of discrimination go so deep that social and economic disparities are deeply intertwined, although in increasingly complex ways. In this imperfect world, none of the proposed solutions is perfect either: the choice is between imperfect instruments with different degrees of effectiveness. That is why we still need reservations for different groups in higher education—not because they are the perfect instruments to rectify long-standing discrimination, but because they are still the most workable method to move in this direction. And most of all, because the nature of Indian society ensures that without such measures, social discrimination and exclusion will only persist and be strengthened.

Jayati Ghosh,
Economic and Political Weekly,
June 17, 2006.

- Castes/classes where the percentage of married women below 17 is 25 percent above the state average in rural areas and 10 percent in urban areas; and that of married men is 10 percent and 5 percent above the state average in rural and urban areas respectively.

- Castes/classes where participation of females in work is at least 25 percent above the state average.

Educational

- Castes/classes where the number of children in the age group of 5 to 15 years who never attended school is at least 25 percent above the state average.

- Castes/classes where the rate of student drop-out in the age group of 5–15 years is at least 25 percent above the state average.

- Castes/classes amongst whom the proportion of matriculates is at least 25 percent below the state average

Economic

- Castes/classes where the average value of family assets is at least 25 percent below the state average.

- Castes/classes where the number of families living in kachcha houses [made of natural, nondurable materials] is at least 25 percent above the state average.

- Castes/classes where the source of drinking water is beyond half a kilometer for more than 50 percent of the households.

- Castes/classes where the number of the households having taken a consumption loan is at least 25 percent above the state average.

Reservation Will Benefit the Disadvantaged

In the Supreme Court judgement on creamy layer, it has been explicitly stated in paragraph 85 "No objection can be taken to the validity and relevancy of the criteria adopted by the

Mandal Commission." It has directed the government to identify creamy layer among the OBCs and ensure that they do not garner all the benefits of reservation.

The committee defined the 'creamy layer' as when a person has been able to shed off the attributes of social and educational backwardness and has secured employment or has engaged himself in some trade/profession of high status and at which stage he is normally in no need of reservation. Thus according to this definition children of: (i) persons holding Constitutional posts, (ii) of persons in service category Group A/Class I, Group B/Class II officials and employees holding equivalent posts in PSUs [Public Sector Undertakings], Banks, Insurance, organisations, universities and private employment (iii) personnel from armed forces and para military forces above the rank of colonel including navy and air force, (iv) persons in professional class, trade business and industry (v) persons holding irrigated agricultural land more than 85 percent of the statutory ceiling area (vi) plantation owners (vii) holders of vacant land and/or buildings in urban areas and urban agglomerations and (viii) persons having an annual income of above Rs 2.5 lakh or possessing wealth above the exemption limit prescribed in the wealth act are excluded from the purview of reservations.

If the opponents of reservation still feel that only the better off will somehow avail the reservation opportunities then they should suggest means to stop this and not cry hoarse over reservations per se. If they believe that reservations are against equality then they should propose an alternate system to replace them. The failure to do so will certainly raise doubts about their notions of equality, which is certainly bereft of social justice.

More Action Is Needed to Ensure Equality

We have been arguing time and again, reservations alone will not solve the whole problem of backwardness. The Mandal

Commission report itself recognises this basic truth and notes: "unless the production relations are radically altered through structural changes and progressive land reforms implemented rigorously all over the country, OBCs will never become truly independent. In view of this, highest priority should be given to radical land reforms by all the states". The class bias of the government too can be understood when it refuses to implement the land reforms agenda in the report and confines itself just to the provision of reservations. The government wants reservations to create an empowered middle class among these sections that lends its voice to the ruling class neo-liberal policies, while it is afraid of land reforms as they weaken the feudal basis of the Indian State.

We in the Left support reservations even though we look at them as a partial remedy because they provide a minimum solace to the deprived sections of our society. The people who avail of reservations and benefit from them should use their knowledge and resources for the interests of the class and sections from which they come and not become the stooges of the ruling classes.

In the era of neo-liberal globalisation, a united fight has to be waged against the policies that are curtailing both educational and employment opportunities. This struggle should demand not only reservations to the backward sections but also strengthening of the public education system and employment opportunities together with the implementation of the land reforms.

> *"The net result is that OBCs [Other Backward Classes] . . . are overwhelmed with an inferiority complex and thus find psychological comfort only in reservations."*

Caste-Based Reservations Reinforce Prejudice

M.R. Venkatesh

M.R. Venkatesh argues in the following viewpoint that members of so-called Other Backward Classes (OBCs) have not been oppressed and exploited as many have claimed. In fact, he posits, many have attended schools and become famous leaders. For these reasons, he concludes, OBCs do not need nor should they have reservations. On the contrary, he opines, continuing to divide Indians by caste furthers the caste system, traps people in lower castes, and perpetuates feelings of inferiority and guilt. Venkatesh is a chartered accountant in Chennai who specializes in business and economic issues.

As you read, consider the following questions:

1. In the author's assertion, who robbed the OBCs of their power, wealth, and status?

2. Who are two people in early history that Venkatesh uses as examples of the OBCs' glorious past?

3. What does the author predict would happen if the supply of education increased?

To rule India—with her huge size and population—the British hit upon a simple yet brilliant idea: divide and rule, with the State playing the crucial role of an arbitrator between various warring groups.

The government of Independent India is largely a remnant of the British Raj with one crucial addition: the ruling elite, comprising Marxists and pseudo-Marxists, largely understands the collective psyche of Indians far better than our colonial oppressors. After all, poverty of ideas invariably leads to politics of poverty.

Accordingly, subsequent governments in India have first ensured shortages, and then played Santa by rationing the insufficient. Quotas fall in this genre.

The Caste System Is Born

Having adopted this paradigm of governance, it was necessary for the Government of India to turn the majority against the minority, Muslims and Christians were to be pitched against Hindus, the 'higher' castes against 'lower' castes, the OBCs [Other Backward Classes] against the MBCs (Most Backward Classes), the BCs [Backward Castes] against the Dalits, the Hindi-speaking against the non-Hindi speaking and so on and so forth.

Else, a system that was predominantly modelled on the lines of the British style of governance—highly centralised, with little accountability—would be unworkable in India. And given this broad idea of dividing Indians, the caste system in India was an obvious candidate.

It may be noted that by the early 20th century the British had already begun dividing the nation on these lines—forwards and backwards. The governments in independent India merely carried the British agenda forward.

One of the popular assumptions built by the British and nurtured subsequently by Marxists about castes is that it is hierarchical and creates a rigid and vertical social structure. And that justified reservations, first for the Dalits (who are not the subject matter of this discussion) and subsequently extended to the backward castes—OBCs.

The nature of competitive populism in contemporary politics makes it extremely difficult even for a cursory discussion on backward castes, their composition and genesis of their backwardness. On the contrary, every government aided and abetted by a pliable media, biased intellectuals and an indifferent public have repeatedly suppressed, distorted or de-legitimised scholarly studies about OBCs.

The truth needs to be told, facts debated and our assumptions re-calibrated.

No One Believes They Are of a Backward Caste

Whether caste is associated with vertical hierarchy or not has been the subject of great study by many historians, analysts and sociologists. 'Interrogating Castes,' a study of Dipankar Gupta, an eminent scholar and historian of great repute, shows that no caste considers itself to be lower in status, when compared with other castes.

In his essay, Gupta recalls an encounter with a 'low caste' woman who claimed that her caste was really Rajput—a higher caste—and was turned into a lower caste after a defeat in war.

Gupta further adds, "This encounter nearly twenty years ago led me to wonder how many low castes have elevated opinions about their caste origins. A new world was revealed to me as I read account after account of those who are customarily called low castes denying their lowly pedigree. Sometimes they said that were Brahmans of a certain kind, on many occasions they claimed Kshatriya status."

Stumped? Read on.

Arun Shourie, in his latest book—*Falling Over Backwards*—reveals something sensational. He quotes two Census Superintendents of the 1931 census who state, 'The feature of interest is that the claim is always for a more dignified title, for admission to a higher caste or exclusion from a caste which is considered low in the social scale.' Shourie further goes on enumerate repeatedly all through this book as to how Sainis and Malis wanted to be classified as Saini Rajputs, Gabits as Marathas, Bedas as Naiks, Blacksmiths as Panch Brahmans, Barias as Kshatriyas, Talpadas as Padhiar Rajputs, Devalis and Bhavins as Naik Marathas . . . the list seems endless, and Shourie's scholarly attempt is replete with such examples of the so-called lower castes seeking a higher caste appellation.

Surprised? Read on.

Lower Castes or Elite Ruling Class?

The late Gandhian, Dharampalji through a painstaking study spread over several decades in India, England and Germany established that before the British rule in India, over two-thirds—yes, two-thirds!—of the Indian rulers belonged to what is today known as the OBCs and conclusively proved that it was the British and not the upper castes who robbed the OBCs of their power, wealth and status.

Dharampalji also exploded the popularly held belief that most of those attending schools must have belonged to the upper castes and again with reference to the British records, proved that the truth was other way round. For instance, during 1822–1825 the share of the Brahman students in indigenous schools in Tamil-speaking areas accounted for 13 per-

The Caste System and the Stages of Life in Hinduism

The pattern of social classes in Hinduism is called the "caste system." The chart shows the major divisions and contents of the system. Basic caste is called varn.a, or "color." Subcaste, or jâti, "birth, life, rank," is a traditional subdivision of varn.a.

		Class	Color
Varnas:	**Twice Born:**	Brahmins Priests and Teachers	White
		Kṣatriyas Warriors and Rulers	Red
		Vaiśyas Farmers, Merchants, Artisans, etc.	Brown
		Śudras Laborers	Black
Outcastes:		Untouchables Polluted Laborers	

TAKEN FROM: Kelley L. Ross, "The Caste System and the Stages of Life in Hinduism," 2005. www.fresian.com.

cent in South Arcot to some 23 percent in Madras, while the OBCs accounted for 70 percent in Salem and Tirunelveli and 84 percent in South Arcot.

Shocked? Another study by Christophe Jaffrelot, a French scholar—*India's Silent Revolution: the Rise of the Low Castes in North Indian Politics*—corroborates the findings of late Dharampalji.

While the subject of the book may be out of context to the discussion on hand, the matter of interest to the extant debate is the historical perspective provided on the status of OBCs in 19th and early 20th century. Some of the important factors highlighted in the book with respect to OBCs are:

All available historical evidence shows that almost none of the OBCs considered themselves to be backward, in any sense of the term, at least till the beginning of the 20th century.

Most of the rulers, both at the local as well as larger regional levels in different regions of India during 16–18th centuries, seem to have come from these OBCs.

Further, most of the professions that sustained the vibrant economy of India, which was considered a great agricultural and industrial nation till early 19th century, were peopled and managed mostly by these communities.

The de-industrialisation of India by the British and the subsequent suspension of all local support systems led to widespread deprivation among all sections of Indian society, notably the OBCs.

Four scholars, perhaps with differing ideologies have arrived at similar conclusions. Yet, look at the specious arguments that have fashioned our debate on this issue.

Look what have we done to ourselves.

The net impact of the above is that we have turned OBCs—the supplicants in the 18th and 19th centuries—into applicants for posts of clerks in government offices, thanks to the reservation policy.

This would be perhaps true of earlier historical periods also. And most of them—from Lord Rama to Krishna, from Maharana Ranjit Singh to Chhatrapati Shivaji to Veerapandia Kattabomman—would in the scheme of our government invariably fall in one of the two categories: OBCs or MBCs!

Due to a conspiracy of coincidences, OBCs seem to have forgotten their glorious past. What else would explain their behaviour of being on all fours before successive governments—and to curry favours? Today they are so used to the standard arguments of being exploited by forward castes (FCs), leave alone OBCs, even the FCs are loathe to buy contrary arguments.

A Purposeful Shortage of Educational Institutions

The net result is that OBCs on the one hand are overwhelmed with an inferiority complex and thus find psychological comfort only in reservations. On the other hand, the upper castes, tutored through tortured history, live constantly in a guilt complex of having wronged their OBC brethren.

In short, our population comprises people who live either on guilt or on an inferiority complex—what a wonderful combination to challenge the world!

Significantly, this is a perfect setting for our politicians, especially the Marxists, to exploit.

All these are pointers to a crucial issue—the manner in which we are governed and the sinister idea of dividing Indians to rule Indians continue in the same manner as the British did to us till Independence.

The Indian politician perfectly understands the system and the Indian psyche. Leveraging the power of the government, our politicians prefer rationing a few thousand seats by constricting demand rather than considering the grand idea of increasing its supply.

For sixty years since Independence, we have one AIIMS, seven IITs and six IIMs [various types of education institutes] for a billion-plus population. Even that tiny speck in the Indian Ocean called Singapore would have more educational institutions for its 4 million population.

Obviously, the idea is to constrict supply and play on the pent up demand. And in the process if history has to be distorted, so be it.

It may be noted that the Marxists would be at hand to lend credibility to any such distortions of history—our silence would be their next ally. Needless to emphasise, it is these distortions of history that rationalize reservations, not the 'historical backwardness' of any castes. But if supply were increased as suggested here, what would our politicians—

Marxists and pseudo Marxists—do? They would simply be jobless, as it would mean end of their brand of politics!

And precisely for these reasons, the current policy of reservations and with it dividing people through castes would continue.

Moral of the story: Without the powerful incentive of reservation every caste in India would be a forward caste.

> *"The Indian government admitted to 12.7 million child laborers in 2001, an increase of about one million in a decade."*

Children in India Are Exploited

Bruce Stokes

In the following viewpoint Bruce Stokes details what he calls the horrors of child labor in India. Overworked and sometimes beaten, millions of children are exploited despite child labor being outlawed in India, the author alleges. Stokes blasts myths that child labor is necessary to support poor families. In actuality, he asserts, child labor brings in a fraction of the pay adults make and it denies children the opportunity for education. As a columnist for the National Journal, *Stokes writes on international economics and foreign relations.*

As you read, consider the following questions:

1. According to the author, how did the New Delhi embroidery factory owner respond to the father who wanted to take his son home?

2. How does Stokes explain his view that children working to support the family is a bad bargain?

3. In what way has Brazil served as a model for eradicating child labor, in the author's opinion?

The sweet-smiling young boy wearing a knit cap and rag wool sweater seemed small for his age. But then, he had lived a harder life than most 12-year-olds. Raised on the streets of rural India, at age 8 he was sold by his aunt to a banker in Delhi to work as a house servant. For four years the youngster was on call 18 hours a day, scrubbing pots and cleaning rooms, one of the tens of thousands of Indian children now working as domestics, the new face of child labor in this country.

"The growing Indian middle class has brought this disaster to the lives of the nation's children," said Kailash Satyarthi, chairman of India's Global March Against Child Labor. As soon as they can afford them, Indian families want servants as a sign of their newfound status. And the cheapest and most docile workers available are boys and girls.

This particular child, whose identity was withheld to protect his privacy, is free now, liberated by one of Mr. Satyarthi's raid-and-rescue teams. He lives with about three dozen other former child laborers at the Mukti ashram on the outskirts of India's capital. Here they receive schooling and counseling until they can be reunited with their families.

Like millions of migrants before him, this young boy has no desire to return to his village. Despite the hardship he has endured, he loves the city. And, typical of all children his age, he dreams. He wants to grow up to be a pilot, despite having only six months of education.

The Horrors of Child Labor

As unrealistic as his dream may be, it is better than the nightmare of child labor that still traps millions of other Indian children, despite a 2006 law that makes it illegal to employ anyone under the age of 14. India still has more children working than any other single country.

Another slight, dark-haired 12-year-old boy, also at the ashram, knows the horrors of child labor all too well. For the last three years he embroidered suits and saris, working 16-hour days, six and a half days a week alongside two dozen other children ages 8 to 16 in a New Delhi factory. He slept at his work bench. And, he claims, he was regularly beaten when his embroidery did not satisfy the owner.

"In time," the boy recalled, "my father came to the factory and asked that I be sent home. But the factory owner refused. He said 'he has been eating a lot and you have to pay for his sleeping arrangement, so I won't send him home.'" Eventually, Mr. Satyarthi's team liberated him, too. And the family was given 1,500 rupees, about $35, for the boy's three years of work.

These boys are two of millions of child laborers around the world. The exact number is probably unknowable. It depends on the definition of childhood and the definition of work.

"Childhood is an evolving concept," said Mr. Satyarthi. The legal age of work varies from country to country. And, when it comes to farm work and family handicraft businesses, experts differ over where to draw the line between exploitative labor and children simply helping out.

In 2004, the International Labor Organization [ILO] guesstimated there were 218 million child laborers worldwide, seven in 10 of them working in agriculture. That figure was down by 11 percent from 2000.

The Indian government admitted to 12.7 million child laborers in 2001, an increase of about one million in a decade. Child labor opponents claim the real total is more than double that figure.

In part, the increase and the discrepancy reflect the prevalence of domestic servitude, which is on the rise as Indian incomes improve. The 2001 government study estimated there were only 185,000 domestic child workers. Activists claim the number is much higher, arguing that domestic child labor is particularly hard to document. Children work privately one and two to the household, not publicly by the dozens in factories. And many are quite young. A recent study in the southern city of Chennai found that a quarter of child domestic workers began working before they were nine. More than 80 percent were girls.

"The law is being flouted behind every other door," said Mr. Satyarthi.

Misconceptions About Child Labor

Such child labor persists, in part, because of widespread misperceptions about its economic necessity and social benefits.

- Myth 1: The prevalence of child labor is an unfortunate consequence of poverty. Not always so. Sri Lanka has a per capita income of $4,100 and 15 percent of its children work. India has a $2,700 per capita income but only 6 percent of Indian children are economically active. Poor societies don't have to have child labor.

- Myth 2: Children need to work to support their families. Indian surveys show that parents do send their children to work believing it will help sustain the family. But it's a bad bargain. ILO studies find that children earn about one-fifth what adults are paid for the same work, so a child's contribution is minimal at best. Moreover, premature work denies children the opportunity to acquire the skills they need to earn decent incomes as adults, undermining their ability to care for their parents in their old age. Sending one's child to work is both economically irrational and shortsighted.

- Myth 3: Curbing child labor hurts employment. "Almost all children who work belong to those families

India's Child Trafficking Statistics

According to the National Human Rights Commission (NHRC), every year an average of 44,476 children go missing in India. Of these, 11,008 are never traced.

The NHRC, in its report "Action Research on Trafficking in Women and Children in India" (2002–2003), suggests that many of the missing children are not really missing but are instead trafficked. Most end up in forced adoptions and marriages, child labour markets or working in the entertainment industry, of which sex tourism is the most recent aspect.

According to figures provided by the National Crime Records Bureau, in 2004, as many as 2,265 cases of kidnapping and abduction of children qualified as forms of trafficking and were reported to the police. Of these, 1,593 cases were of kidnapping for marriage, 414 were for illicit sex, 92 for unlawful activity, 101 for prostitution and the rest for various other things such as slavery, begging and even selling body parts. Most of these children (72 percent) were between 16 and 18 years of age. Twenty-five percent were children aged 11–15 years.

Irish Times, *May 26, 2007.*

where the parents can't find jobs for more than 100 days a year," said Mr. Satyarthi. So many children may be taking jobs from their own parents. Despite the recent decline in child labor in India's carpet industry, thanks to better enforcement of labor laws and the consequent increase in labor costs, carpet exports are up and the jobs are being filled by able-bodied adults. Countries can have more jobs without employing more children.

- Myth 4: Children are better suited for some work than adults. This "nimble fingers" argument is widely believed. But an ILO study of over 2,000 weavers found that children were no more likely than adults to have the dexterity to tie the finest carpet knots. They can just be paid less.

- Myth 5: Child labor is a valuable part of early childhood education. Studies in Brazil demonstrate that entering the workforce before age 13 can actually lower adult lifetime earnings by up to 17 percent. Children learn best at a desk, not at a loom.

Clearly, the eradication of child labor need not await the eradication of poverty.

Activism Is Needed

Brazil has shown the way. For more than a decade Brasilia has paid parents a small stipend—$4.50 a month per child—to send their kids to school rather than to work. More than a million children now participate in the program.

The ILO estimates that it would cost $38 billion a year for 20 years to eliminate child labor. Washington has already contributed more than $20 million to an Indian program to eliminate children from the most hazardous industries. More such investments are justified. Studies show the economic benefits of such spending outweigh the costs by nearly 6 to 1.

In Europe and the United States child labor did not disappear thanks to the elimination of poverty. It was eradicated once activists pressured governments to enforce the law and to create educational opportunities for all children. That same struggle is now ongoing in India. History suggests that outside pressure and financial aid can help.

"Child labor is a denial of childhood," said Mr. Satyarthi. "It's the denial of their future participation in the economy. This must end. And it is nonnegotiable."

Periodical Bibliography

The following articles have been selected to supplement the diverse views presented in this chapter.

Flavia Agnes — "Domestic Violence Act, A Portal of Hope," *Combat Law*, November–December 2005.

Neera Chandhoke — "Three Myths About Reservations," *Economic and Political Weekly*, June 10, 2006.

Anuj Chopra — "New Protection Against Domestic Violence in India," *Christian Science Monitor*, March 8, 2007.

Pamela Constable — "Muslims in India 'Targeted with Suspicion,'" *Washington Post*, August 14, 2006.

The Economist — "The Cross They Bear," February 7, 2008.

Feminazisofindia — "Save Indian Family Foundation Calls on the Nation to Observe Black Day," Feminist Media, October 21, 2008. http://feministmedia.wordpress.com.

Salil Kader — "Social Stratification Among Muslims in India," Countercurrents.org, June 15, 2004.

Surendra K. Kaushik — "Do Not Reinforce Two Indias," *Business Week*, November 2, 2006.

Andy Mukherjee — "The Curse of the Caste Haunts India Inc.," *International Herald Tribune*, April 25, 2006.

Press Trust of India — "Caste-Based Reservations Have Helped Human Development in South India: Book," July 1, 2007.

V. Kumara Swamy — "The Abuse of Dowry Law," *Telegraph* (Calcutta), July 30, 2008.

CHAPTER 4

What Efforts Would Ensure India's Future Success?

Chapter Preface

Marriage is the cornerstone of Indian society. Most unions are arranged by parents for their children, sometimes at birth. Traditional Indian weddings last a week and involve elaborate ceremonies with matching garb and silk turbans with real feathers and jewels. Dowries, sometimes including diamonds, cars, and cash in the case of the rich, are often given from the bride's family to the groom's, though this practice has been outlawed. The new couple then moves in together with the husband's parents and extended family. This all serves to cement the matrimony, which is seen as a religious contract between families; and it is eternal—the Hindi language does not even have a word for divorce. Today, however, all this is changing. While in 1990 less than eight marriages out of one thousand ended in divorce in India, now the rates have skyrocketed. Two of five couples married in Mumbai since 2002 have petitioned for divorce. Experts argue over what is causing the changing landscape and what this means for families.

Many claim that these statistics portend the widespread breakdown of families and traditional values. "The great Indian family is definitely under threat," warns Shobhaa Dé, author of *Spouse: The Truth About Marriage*. Some blame Western influences via movies and the Internet for challenging India's traditional views of marriage. *Washington Post* writer Emily Wax confirms, "Older Indians still view divorce as a societal ill imported from the West." To some observers, broken marriages represent a threat not only to families but to the entire country. Since family is a fundamental unit of society, the breakdown of families demonstrates a "weakening in the fabric of the society," according to Sam George, author of *Understanding the Coconut Generation*. "When a society grows weaker," he opines, "soon it begins to show in the national character." In his view, lack of strength and commitment on the family level extends far beyond.

Not everyone laments India's rising divorce rates, though. Interestingly, some intellectuals hail it as a sign that the country is making gains. Journalist Amit Varma maintains, "Every divorce means that two people have a better chance at finding Hindu practice of sati, for example, a recent widow is willingly or forcibly burned alive on her husband's funeral pyre." Many call it the ultimate crime against women. Although sati was outlawed in the 1800s, a prevention act had to be passed as recently as 1987 because the practice still occurred. The act was protested by people who maintain it is a woman's right to commit sati, which they believe symbolizes a wife's virtuousness and eternal devotion to her husband. A more widespread issue that's considered a violation of women's rights is domestic violence. According to a United Nations Population Fund report, as many as seven in ten wives in the country have endured beatings or rape at home, which inflicts physical and psychological damage and reduces their productivity in the workplace. Laws protecting Indian women from abuse are often opposed by men's groups and traditionalists who argue that the legislation unfairly promotes women and gives them too much power.

This idea that one group's privileges come at the expense of another's makes the issue of rights especially thorny. How to balance the rights of many differing groups in India is the topic of debate in the following chapter. The obstacles encountered by minorities in India are not easily overcome, but gradually India's minority citizens are progressing toward equality.

"The people of India . . . are secular and tolerant and desire communal harmony and better inter-religious relations."

Secularism Will Prevail in India

Asghar Ali Engineer

Tolerance for differing cultures and religions has been the basis of Indian society for centuries, according to Asghar Ali Engineer in the following viewpoint. In his opinion, secularism faltered when a political party with an interest in promoting Hinduism came to power, but was restored once a new party took over. Indians want communal violence to end, he asserts. Secularism will be boosted, in the author's prediction, by increasing numbers of lower caste voters, globalization, and better education and opportunities for Muslims. Engineer is an Islamic scholar and human rights activist who has published over forty books.

As you read, consider the following questions:

1. What distinction does Engineer make regarding clashes that give rise to unrest and communal tensions in society?

Asghar Ali Engineer, "Future of Communal Relations in India," *Secular Perspective*, October 16-31, 2006. Copyright © 2006, CENTER FOR STUDY OF SOCIETY AND SECULARISM. Reproduced by permission.

2. What does the author say the Gujarat carnage diverted attention from in 2002, as an example of ruling classes resorting to communal-based politics?

3. According to the author, why are communal forces losing credibility with Indians?

What is the future of communal relations in India? What will be the likely scenario in coming 30 years? This is an important question. Is India doomed as a secular democracy? Or does India's future lie in secular democracy? Will the Hindutva forces gain or lose? There are different answers to these questions, which is quite natural. In complex social and political problems there are no easy answers. To get some probable answers one has to get at the root of the problem.

India, it is important to note, has been a multi-religious, multi-cultural and multi-lingual society for centuries. Forces of tolerance have always been strong in its soil. Besides others Emperors Ashoka and Akbar have been great symbols of tolerance and openness to other religions. Throughout medieval ages, one hardly finds instances of inter-communal clashes though among religious priesthood there was bigotry and sectarianism. This bigotry and sectarianism as exposed by poets like Kabir.

However, the Sufi and Bhakti movements acted as bridge builders. They effectively countered the narrow mindedness of priestly class and spread love and humanism. The Sufi and Bhakti saints, were more spiritual than religious in ritualistic sense. Their whole emphasis was on love, peace and harmony. They had their roots among common people, poor and of lowly origin. They kept their distance from rulers and ruling classes.

The Partition of India

It is important to note that it is clash of interests, which brings about unrest and communal tensions in society, not clash of religions. Religions do not clash; it is vested interests, which do. In medieval ages religious communities were not politically organised, they were distinctly different yet not hostile to each other as they did not cater to political needs.

It is with the event of colonialism on one hand, and, subsequent parliamentary democracy that led to politicisation of religion and religious communities. Thus inter-religious clashes are in fact, inter-political clashes. Different political parties carve out their vote-banks among different religious communities and target some community, in order to emerge as champion of one's own community. In fact, they are champions of their own political interests, rather than community's interests.

In India such communal division occurred mainly due to colonial machinations. It ultimately led to division of our motherland. This political vivisection became a running sore for people of India, particularly for those of majority community as they saw Muslims as responsible for division of the country. Muslims as a community were not responsible for division but only a section of upper class Muslim elite in collaboration with British colonial power brought about this division. In fact common Muslims are really suffering today on account of this division.

The rightwing Hindu politicians exploited the issue of partition to the hilt with an eye to Hindu votes and often incited communal violence. This violence intensified during the decade of eighties in post-independence India. Most of the major riots in independent India took place during 1980 to 1992–93. There are number of reasons for this. By the time we saw dawn of eighties about 40 years had passed since India became independent. The democratic processes intensified and brought more democratic awareness among the minorities and weaker sections of India and they got better organised by then to demand their due share in power.

The Rise and Fall of the BJP

The upper caste Hindus felt that in coming years they will have to yield more and more share of power to minorities and low caste Hindus (dalits) and hence the Bhartiya Janata Party (BJP), mainly representing the political and economic interests of upper caste Hindu elite, raised alarm and began propaganda blast against minorities and dalits and led to heightened inter-communal and inter-caste tensions. The BJP used Ram Temple controversy as a powerful symbol to mobilise Hindu votes and ultimately rode to power in 1999 and remained in power until 2004.

The Sangh Parivar (which includes Rashtriya Seva Sangh, Vishwa Hindu parishad and BJP) tried to weaken secularism and Hinduise Indian plot during their rule. It was during the BJP rule (both at the Centre as well as in Gujarat state) that Gujarat carnage took place in 2002, which officially 1000 and unofficially 2000 Muslims were brutally killed. Thus inter-religious violence achieved its climax during the BJP rule, which bases its politics on hatred of minority communities.

It was during the BJP rule that attacks against miniscule minority of Christians also began. An Australian Christian priest James Staines, working for lepers among tribals in a distant village of Orissa in Eastern India was burnt to death along with his two young children. Many other Christian priests and nuns were also attacked or murdered. This was the darkest period of secular India.

But it is to be noted that people of India rejected the BJP rule because of its communal excesses and voted the UPA (United Progressive Alliance) government led by the Congress to power in the elections of 2004. Thus the people of India once again proved that they are secular and tolerant and desire communal harmony and better inter-religious relations. Though one cannot see inter-communal relations in straight line as much depends on political dynamics in the country.

Is India a Secular State?

Looking at the various constitutional provisions, the answer is 'Yes'. The ideals of secular state have clearly been embodied under the Indian Constitution and the provisions are being implemented in substantial measure. But the circumstances after independence have posed a challenge before secularism of India for a number of times. Sometimes it is also alleged that by Uniform Civil Code, the existence of minorities in India is in danger or it is an assault on the identity of minorities. India being still a traditional society that contains not one, but many traditions owing their origin in part to the different religions that exist here. While India carries with it many traditions it has managed to retain the secular character of its polity, while in many countries especially from the third world, a secular authority has crumbled in face of conflicting traditions.

Tarun Arora, "Secularism Under the Constitutional Framework of India," LegalServicesIndia.com.

Emotionalised, Communalised Politics

However, on the whole, it can be said that common people of India are desirous of peaceful co-existence and do not appreciate communal turmoil in the country. The dark side of economic development is vast poverty-stricken underbelly of India. India is still at 137th place out of 139 countries surveyed as far as malnutrition and deaths caused by hunger is concerned. Such stark poverty cannot but have political implications.

The ruling classes use caste and communal issues to divert attention from such horrific problems. Many politicians are tempted to resort to communal-based, instead of issue-based politics. The Gujarat carnage of 2002 took place precisely when the BJP Government was signing various international trade treaties and liberalising economy benefiting handful of economic elite.

Thus in coming 30 years one cannot expect smooth inter-caste and inter-communal relations as the ruling classes would certainly tempted to employ emotional issues to catch votes of common people without solving their problems. This process of emotionalising and communalising politics is aided and abated by the media also, as media itself is controlled by political and economic elite.

The Sangh Parivar has consolidated its base during six years of its rule and possesses disciplined cadre and thus possesses great capacity to communalise politics and provoke communal violence. But there are countervailing forces too which go in favour of more secularized democracy.

Factors That Are Strengthening Secularism

The lower castes (dalits) though at times get used by upper caste Hindus and are swept off their feet by powerful emotional propaganda but on the whole tend to be anti-Sangh Parivar force. These dalits are main victims of upper caste elite politics and their leaders try to counter communal politics in order to keep their caste flock with them. The caste awareness is increasing with spread of education among dalits and with spread of democratic awareness. Though dalits and minorities are far behind in the field of education, yet more and more are getting educated and are becoming aware of their political rights. Greater the political awareness among dalits and OBCs (other backward classes), more challenging it would be for communal politicians to manipulate religious and communal sentiments.

Another factor is increasing globalisation, which in itself creates contradictory effects as far as communal situation is concerned. On one hand it intensifies urge for religious and cultural identities to face homogenizing global processes and on the other, it opens up economic opportunities for educated middle classes and induces their out-migration thus reducing communal potentialities.

It is also interesting to note that today there is increased awareness among Muslims in India to make a concerted effort to better their position through more education and better economic opportunities and avoid emotional issues which bring nothing but disaster for them. They were entangled in Ramjanambhoomi politics and suffered a great deal. Thus with few exceptions, Muslims are shedding their communal past, and preparing themselves for better future prospects.

Also, communal forces are losing credibility among people of India. They have no achievement to show except communal rhetoric and bloodshed. Before coming to power they claimed to be 'clean' and non-corrupt. However, now many corruption scandals are coming out in which their leaders were involved during their rule. On this count also, they have lost much ground.

Thus in coming 30 years, it appears, communal forces will find it very difficult to regain their lost ground and communal politics will be weakened. However, much will depend on performance of secular forces also. Communal forces thrive more due to failure of secular forces than on account of their inherent strength. Communal forces gain strength only because secular forces fail to assert and perform. Communal forces, it appears, will lose ground and one will see greater urge among people for co-existence and harmonious living in coming thirty years.

> *"For all its professions of secularism, the Indian state has not developed a stance of either equal indifference to or equal respect for all the ... religions."*

Secularism Is Faltering in India

Meera Nanda

Meera Nanda contends in the following viewpoint that Indians are growing more religious and that this religiosity is spreading to the public sphere. In her assertions, this challenges notions of secularism. More Indians are partaking in rituals and pilgrimages, the author maintains, and globalization is helping to spread ideals of Hindu nationalism. Nanda asserts that Hinduism in particular has been injected into government speeches and events. Nanda authored the forthcoming book God and Globalization in India, *from which the viewpoint is adapted.*

As you read, consider the following questions:

1. According to statistics cited by the author, what percentage of trips are taken for religious reasons?

2. How does Nanda describe "Vedic sciences"?

Meera Nanda, "Rush Hour of the Gods," *New Humanist*, vol. 123, March-April 2008. Copyright © 2008 The Rationalist Association. Reproduced by permission.

3. What is deepening a sense of Hindu chauvinism and widening the chasm between Hindus and non-Hindus, in the author's assertion?

"The world today is as furiously religious as it ever was. . . . Experiments with secularized religions have generally failed; religious movements with beliefs and practices dripping with reactionary supernaturalism have widely succeeded."

—*Peter Berger, Desecularization of the World*

Those looking for evidence to back Peter Berger's conclusion can do no better than take a closer look at the religious landscape of India, the "crouching tiger" of 21st-century global capitalism.

India today is teeming with millions of educated, relatively well-to-do men and women who enthusiastically participate in global networks of science and technology. The Indian economy is betting its fortunes on advanced research in biotechnology and the drug industry, whose very existence is a testament to the naturalistic and disenchanted understanding of the natural world. And yet a vast majority of these middle-class beneficiaries of modern science and technology continue to believe in supernatural powers supposedly embodied in idols, "god-men" or "god-women," stars and planets, rivers, trees and sacred animals. By all indications, they treat supernatural beings and powers with utmost earnestness and reverence and go to great lengths to please them in the hopes of achieving their desires.

According to the 2007 State of the Nation survey conducted by the Centre for the Study of Developing Societies among Indians, the level of religiosity has gone up considerably in the past five years [2003–2008]. A mere five percent of respondents said that their religious belief had declined, while 30 percent said they had become more religious. The same poll found that education and exposure to modern urban life seem to make Indians more, not less, religious: "Urban educated Indians are more religious than their rural and illiterate counterparts . . . religiosity has increased more in small towns and cities than in villages."

Another measurable indicator of rising religiosity is the tremendous rise in pilgrimages or religious tourism. According to a recent study by the National Council for Applied Economic Research, "religious trips account for more than 50 percent of all package tours, much higher than leisure tour packages at 28 percent." The most recent figures show that in 2004, more than 23 million people visited the Lord Balaji temple at Tirpuati, while 17.25 million trekked to the mountain shrine of Vaishno Devi. Here I will focus on Hindus, who make up nearly 85 percent of India's population. But they are not the only ones who are becoming more religious: indicators of popular religiosity are rising among Indian Muslims, Christians and Sikhs as well.

Religion Is Changing with the Times

Today's generation of Indian upper and middle classes are not content with the deritualised, slimmed-down, philosophised or secular humanist version of Hinduism that appealed to the earlier generation of elites. They are instead looking for "jagrit" or awake gods who respond to their prayers and who fulfill their wishes—the kind of gods that sociologists Rodney Starke and Roger Finke, authors of *Acts of Faith*, describe as "personal, caring, loving, merciful, close, accessible . . . all of which can be summed up in a belief that 'there is someone up there who cares.'" The textual or philosophical aspects of Sanskritic Hinduism have by no means diminished in cultural prestige: they continue to serve as the backdrop of "Vedic sciences" (as Hindu metaphysics is sold these days), and continue to attract a loyal following of spiritual seekers from India and abroad. But what is changing is simply that it is becoming fashionable to be religious and to be seen as being religious. The new elites are shedding their earlier reticence about openly participating in religious rituals in temples and in public ceremonies like kathas and yagnas. If anything, the ritual dimension is becoming more public and more ostentatious.

Not only are rituals getting more elaborate but many village and working-class gods and goddesses are being adopted by the middle classes, business elites and non-resident Indians—a process of Sanskritisation that has been called a "gentrification of gods". Worship of local gods and goddesses that until recently were associated with the poor, illiterate and lower castes is finding a new home in swank new suburbs with malls and multiplexes. The enormous growth in the popularity of the goddess called Mariamman or Amma in the south and Devi or Mata in the rest of the country is a case in point. . . .

On the face of it, contemporary popular Hinduism appears to be the very epitome of a dynamic and inventive religious tradition which is changing to keep pace with the changing time. Clearly, all the new gods, god-men/god-women, new temples and rituals add up to an impressive inventory of creative innovations that are allowing men and women to take their gods with them as they step into the heady, though unsettling, world dominated by global corporate capitalism. But there is an underside: the same innovations in religious ritual and dogmas that are enabling the "Great Indian Middle Class" to adjust to global capitalism are also deepening a sense of Hindu chauvinism, and widening the chasm between Hindus and non-Hindu minorities. The banal, everyday Hindu religiosity is simultaneously breeding a banal, everyday kind of Hindu ultra-nationalism. This kind of nationalism is not openly proclaimed in fatwas, nor does it appear on the election manifestos of political parties. Its power lies in structuring the common sense of ordinary people.

The net result is a new kind of political and nationalistic Hinduism which is invented out of old customs and traditions that people are fond of and familiar with. Because it builds upon deeply felt religiosity, it sucks in even those who are not particularly anti-Muslim or anti-Christian. Religious festivals, temple rituals and religious discourses become so many ways of "flagging" India as a Hindu nation, and India's cultural superiority as due to its Hindu spirituality.

Hindu Gods Used as Props

The best way to describe the banality of Hindu nationalism and the role of religion in it is to show how it works.

The example comes from the recent inauguration of Shri Hari Mandir, a new temple that opened in Porbandar in Gujarat in February 2006. The grand sandstone temple and the priest-training school called Sandipani Vidyaniketan attached to it are a joint venture of the Gujarat government, the business house of the Ambanis and the charismatic guru Rameshbhai Oza. The inauguration ceremony of this temple-gurukul complex provides a good example of how Hindu gods end up serving as props for Hindu nationalism and Hindu supremacy.

According to the description provided by the organisers themselves, the temple was inaugurated by Bharion Singh Shekhawat, the vice-president of the country, with the infamous chief minister Narendra Modi in attendance. Also in attendance were the widow of Dhirubhai Ambani and the rest of the Ambani clan whose generous financial donations had built the temple. Some 50,000 well-heeled devotees of Oza from India and abroad crowded into the temple precincts to watch the event.

The elected representatives of "secular" India, in their official capacity, prayed before the temple idols—something so routine that it hardly evokes a response from anyone anymore. The prayer was followed by the national anthem sung before the gods, followed by recital of the Vedas by the student-priests, followed by a Gujarati folk dance. This was followed by speeches that liberally mixed up the gods and the nation, with quite a bit of rhetoric about the greatness of Hindu "science" thrown in for good measure. Modi, the chief instigator of the 2002 Godhara riots between Hindus and Muslims, spoke glowingly of the "tolerance" and "secularism" of Hinduism. He went on to recommend that yagnas and religious recitals be held all over the country before undertaking any new construction because Hinduism is "inherently ecological". Next came Mrs Ambani, who urged mixing spirituality with industry. The vice-president, in his turn, spoke of how modern and scientific Hindu traditions were, comparing the gods' weapons with modern missiles and their vehicles with modern-day helicopters.

The theme of the superiority of ancient Hindu science was taken up a week later when the president of India, Abdus Kalam, came down to the temple-ashram complex to inaugurate its "science museum", which highlights ancient Hindu discoveries in astronomy/astrology, medicine (ayurveda), architecture (vastu) and such. Without ever questioning what validity the Earth-at-the-centre astronomy/astrology of Aryabhatta has in the modern world, the nuclear physicist president went on to claim not only the greatness of antiquity but also the continued relevance of the ancients for "enriching" modern astronomy. The ancients were smoothly turned into the guiding lights of modern science—regardless of the fact that their cosmology has been falsified by it.

This is representative of how India's state-temple-industrial complex works: the gods become the backdrop, and the traditional puja [a ritualistic form of Hindu worship] the medium, for asserting the Hindu-ness of India and the greatness of both. Worship of the gods becomes indistinguishable from the worship of Hindu culture and the Indian nation. Devotees come to listen to hymns sung to gods, but end up worshipping a political ideology—and cannot tell the difference. The cult of nation, furthermore, is simultaneously turned into a cult of "reason" and "science", without the critical and empirical spirit of science.

The Failure of Secularism

Once the beloved and popular gods become identified with the land and its culture, Hindu nationalism becomes an everyday affair. No one has to pass fatwas and there is no need to launch a militant battle against the West. Hindu nationalists have no use for such crude tools. They would rather turn the worship of gods into the worship of the nation and they would rather beat the West by appropriating the West's strengths in empirical sciences for their own gods. The tragedy is that the religiosity of ordinary believers provides the building blocks for this banal, but far from benign, Hindu nationalism.

Economic globalisation and neo-liberal reforms have created the material and ideological conditions in which a popular and ritualistic Hindu religiosity is growing. Popular religiosity, in turn, is being directed into a mass ideology of Hindu supremacy and Hindu nationalism.

This trend is a symptom of a deeper, more fundamental malaise, namely the failure of secularism. For all its professions of secularism, the Indian state has not developed a stance of either equal indifference to or equal respect for all the many religions of India. It has instead treated the religion of the majority as the civic religion of the Indian nation itself. The result is a deep and widespread Hinduisation of the public sphere, which is only growing under the conditions of globalisation.

> *"Education should be focused . . . on every individual knowing who he is and why he is here."*

India Needs Political and Educational Reform

John R. Thomson

In the following viewpoint, geopolitical analyst and India traveler John R. Thomson suggests that India follow Mahatma Gandhi's vision for the country's future. Gandhi desired honesty in government and all human dealings, and in Thomson's contention, this requires rooting out corruption in India's government and promoting values and good governance. Furthermore, in the author's view, the growth of the country requires that the grade school and higher education systems be revamped. Improvements must be made, he argues, for the education goals for children to be reached and for the country to produce qualified workers.

As you read, consider the following questions:

1. In Thomson's contention, what is a key reason foreign businesspeople do not do business in India?

2. What promising actions is the conglomerate Tata taking that the author predicts will help India?

3. In Thomson's view, what decision made by China will challenge India's lead in regional competition?

P ivotal aspects of [Mohandas, or ahatma] Gandhi's vision for India remain elusive, importantly including honesty in government and all human dealings, citizen involvement in community governance and well-being, and general cleanliness. Indeed, much of what the country has yet to achieve is ultimately reflected in the Gandhi ethos and can be communicated as such.

If the far-fetched concept of a unified, democratic India has been successful, the more mundane requirements to solidify the nation as a major political and economic entity can doubtless be achieved, utilizing the still-vibrant memory of the nation's greatest hero. . . .

There is a palpable need to heighten a sense of pan-Indian responsibility—and destiny—in the spirit of the Mahatma. And that importantly includes coming face to face with the legacy of corruption.

Corruption Abounds

Seasoned international businessmen place Indian bureaucracy in first position for inefficiency and close to the top in corruption, when compared with other countries. Needless demand for forms and approvals daunt the most patient prospective investor, and governmental red tape is a key reason cited by foreign businessmen for deciding *not* to do business in India.

Opinions are divided as to whether government inefficiency and corruption can in fact be significantly reduced, much less eliminated. Far too many Indian and foreign businesses continue to pay for "facilitation" of the complex, multitiered project approval process. As Indians commemorate the sixtieth anniversary of their independence, it is unfortunately fitting to note Mahatma Gandhi's wry observation: "Corruption and hypocrisy ought not to be inevitable products of democracy, as they undoubtedly are today."

The political side of government is as murky as the bureaucratic. At every level, politicians abound who are ready and willing to assist in moving projects forward—and who are equally ready to block a project it not properly "consulted." The Bharatiya Janata Party, the leading opposition party nationally, with strong support from religious Hindus, is no less a stranger to corruption than the Congress Party, which traces its roots to Mahatma Gandhi, or than the communist parties.

Indeed, in recent months D. Raja, national secretary of the Communist Party of India (CPI) has campaigned vociferously against public and private staff reductions and privatization of state activities, including private management of pension funds. Demagogic public outcry and private stalling tactics to the contrary, no one predicts either the CPI or the Communist Party of India (Marxist), known as CPI(M), will give up the perks of coalition power. The bureaucratic miasma is endemic and, so far, there is little concerted effort to rectify it.

Righteousness, Transparency, and Good Governance

Within the private sector, there are encouraging voices who understand the importance of values to economic success and how spirituality remains critical to India's competitiveness, underscoring key aspects of Gandhi's message. P.R. Krishna Kumar, managing director of Arya Vaidya Pharmacy (Coimbatore) Ltd.—a firm specializing in Ayurveda, the 5,000 year-old natural system of mind, body and spiritual care—believes India must regain its moral balance:

> Our country's strength was its great spiritual awareness. Dharma—righteousness—was our greatest asset. Education

should be focused inside, on every individual knowing who he is and why he is here, not just on knowing about everything outside the individual. Today, everything except that is taught.

More positively, Krishna Kumar sees

more and more people and institutions seeking and working on solutions. Indian and foreign companies are increasingly taking the challenge, forming educational and welfare units for their employees and the communities where they operate. There is a steadily growing social awareness.

Some public officials are successfully harnessing that emerging sense of communal responsibility and understand how promoting transparency, good governance and encouraging investment benefit everyone. While a number of communist functionaries have proved adept at little else than commanding headlines, the communist Chief Minister of West Bengal, Buddhadeb Bhattacharjee, has run a successful campaign for major industrial investment. Indian conglomerate Tata—in addition to numerous other domestic and foreign corporations—is investing billions of dollars in Kolkata and other Bengali districts. IBM is adding 3,000 West Bengal employees to its 43,000 national base, as a key part of a $6 billion Indian investment program during the next three years. Historically one of the poorest states in the country, West Bengal currently ranks second only to Gujarat in attracting foreign investment.

But the private sector cannot maintain India on its march to balanced development alone. Unfortunately for progressive governance, the country's two leading communist parties are members of Prime Minister Manhoman Singh's ruling coalition, making progress a stop-and-start affair. This serves as a drag on efforts to modernize and upgrade multiple facets of the country's economy.

An Educational System in Shambles

Nowhere is this more apparent than in the desperate need to reform India's educational system. There is no disagreement among leaders across the society: The country cannot continue its growth without significant overhaul and expansion of academic facilities and curricula from the elementary through the university level. To do so will require extensive investment, and therefore support of and some sacrifice by well-heeled urbanites.

The country has some noteworthy institutions, including the India Institute of Technology, India Institute of Science, and Delhi and Hyderabad Universities, but there is a serious lack of facilities and quality learning at all levels. Domestic and foreign companies alike find filling more than menial positions increasingly difficult. Newspapers run pages of vacancy announcements, regularly publishing special editorial features on the need for skilled manpower.

The state system through grade twelve is in shambles, providing such bad education that although millions of children are unschooled, buildings are closing for lack of students. Scant heed is paid to student attendance and teachers take their salaries but are themselves truant. Most educational materials are sub-par, one English text for Hindi speakers that I looked at was functionally useless. At the same time, independent, privately operated schools abound and an uncounted number of families do without other necessities to provide their children a basic education at these institutions.

Higher-education requirements are somewhat better served by the state, but supply of scats at public and private institutions is far less than demand—despite there being some 18,000 colleges and universities, all but a few are pedagogically deficient.

English fluency and cricket are two of Britain's great legacies, and although India retains its numerical lead in English, regional competition abounds. The call-center business, for-

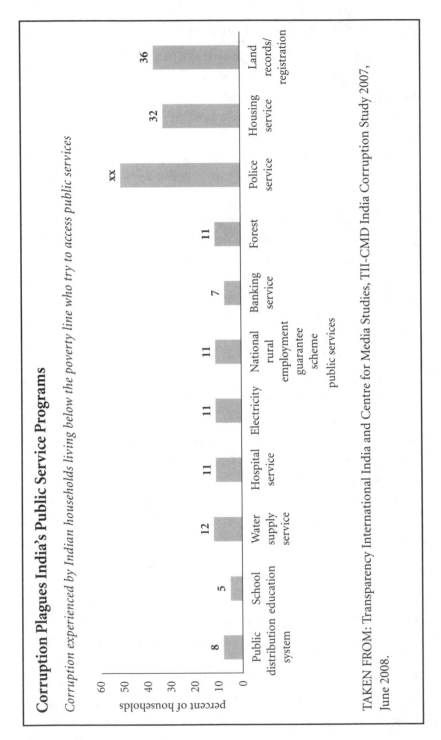

Corruption Plagues India's Public Service Programs

Corruption experienced by Indian households living below the poverty line who try to access public services

percent of households

Public distribution system	School education	Water supply service	Hospital service	Electricity	National rural employment guarantee scheme	Banking service	Forest	Police service	Housing service	Land records/ registration
8	5	12	11	11	11	7	11	xx	32	36

public services

TAKEN FROM: Transparency International India and Centre for Media Studies, TII-CMD India Corruption Study 2007, June 2008.

merly dominated by India, now significantly includes the Philippines, with its strong English-speaking base. A greater challenge, with a major impact to be felt by 2020 and thereafter, is China's decision to make English a compulsory subject. Should China surpass India in English fluency, observers concede that India will be hard-pressed to successfully challenge the giant to its northeast, economically or politically.

Proposed Reforms

Educational reform, in short, cannot come soon enough. Professor Gautam Desiraju of Hyderabad University has sounded the clarion call: "Remedial measures in our science and education sectors need to be taken incisively, swiftly, and almost ruthlessly. Our fatal attraction for incremental changes and consensual thinking has been our undoing" Dr. Desiraju believes "developing 20 good universities with funding at the Chinese levels is not beyond us."

Most debate focuses on each of 17,500 mostly mediocre colleges affiliating with one of the 350 universities, plus accreditation of foreign institutions. While the latter could provide some relief to a chronic shortage of qualified teachers, curriculum restructuring must also be addressed.

Moreover, the first twelve years must be completely restructured. Prime Minister Singh has called for mandatory education through the sixth year, a laudable goal that can only be achieved if facilities, teacher and content issues are solved. "The education system needs to be expanded rapidly at all levels", Dr. Singh believes, and predicts that "the success of our educational initiatives at the grassroots level, along with India's favorable demographics, will ensure that a far greater number pass out of high school each year."

The prime minister, like virtually all informed observers, does not question that jobs will be available for the qualified. The question, rather, is "Can India actually provide sufficiently qualified workers to fuel the ever-expanding demand in the marketplace?" A retired Indian-American professor at a major U.S. university put it this way when visiting his fatherland: "There is no downside to improved education. It is in some ways comparable to what so many countries have learned about lowering taxes. In the case of education, the more and better educated the Indian population, the greater will be India's economic growth and, ultimately, its strength as a nation."

"If we seize this moment, India can transit out of poverty, and coming generations can enjoy an era of unprecedented prosperity."

India Must Make Reformations to Address Poverty and Food Shortages

Robyn Meredith

Robyn Meredith, foreign correspondent for Forbes, *authored* The Elephant and the Dragon: The Rise of India and China and What It Means for All of Us. *In the following excerpt from her book, she argues that to alleviate poverty and boost food production, India must modernize its infrastructure and encourage companies to hire in India. Most Indians live on less than $2 a day, she observes. The construction of roads and job creation on a major scale, she avers, could help them out of poverty. Meredith asserts that India also needs electricity and water to irrigate crops and lower-interest loans for farmers to buy supplies.*

As you read, consider the following questions:

1. What three things is job creation likely to require, in Meredith's prediction?

2. How much of India's fruits and vegetables spoil before reaching markets, according to the author?

3. What pattern does the author say is opposite from that of the United States?

Change has come in small increments to India's villages, where 70 percent of the population lives. Many villages now have a communal television, and those who can afford a computer often have dial-up Internet access, which is helping raise awareness of the world beyond. But time has stood still on many more pressing, day-to-day problems. Many villages still lack running water, electricity, and reliable access to medical care. In 2006, in an effort to cut down on diseases like diarrhea, the government embarked on a high-profile campaign to persuade Indian villagers to install outhouses and stop using nearby fields as toilets. This is the very same hygiene mantra [Mohandas, or Mahatma] Gandhi championed seventy years earlier.

Widespread Poverty

A village in eastern India called Idulbera shows that even villages that have made big gains have not managed to lift residents into the middle class. Negi Singh Sadar, seventy, is the leader of Idulbera, where children tend cows and goats while adults work the fields or travel over bumpy dirt roads to the nearby city of Jamshedpur to look for work. Entire families live in one-room, dirt-floored homes, and the sight of a car or motorcycle is a rarity, despite the eight-mile distance to the nearest city. . . .

Widespread poverty like that found in urban shantytowns and in villages like Idulbera lingers because incomes are rising from such a low base. India's 1991 reforms stimulated overall economic growth, and India's average incomes have nearly doubled in the past decade [1997–2007]. Since then, hundreds of millions of Indians moved up from extreme poverty to the ranks of the merely poor. In Bangalore's biggest slum, Ejipura, huts with plastic sheets for roofs have been upgraded to tiny concrete houses in recent years. Nonetheless, in 2005, about 36 percent of the Indian population still lived on less than one dollar a day and 81 percent on less than two dollars a day, according to the Asian Development Bank.

Still, all the call center jobs in the world wouldn't solve India's poverty problem. . . .

Job Creation for Indians

Bringing India's poor long on the ride to a New India would require vast job creation. That is likely to come only with the addition of thousands of factories, myriad construction projects, or the nurturing of a big increase in agricultural exports—or all three.

A lot depends on how soon India modernizes its infrastructure. Until more roads are built to connect factories and farms with ports and railways, neither factories nor farmers are likely to see a China-style export boom that would create hundreds of millions of jobs. However haltingly, India has finally begun building roads and highways, and that has not only created jobs laying asphalt but also helped connect remote towns and villages to cities. That has enabled some farmers to get produce to markets more efficiently and allowed other villagers to commute to better-paying city jobs. A road-building boom would beget the construction of new factories, but no one can say when this boom will come. Until then, workers will be stuck gaining ground slowly.

Despite the lack of modern infrastructure, India has already seen noticeable gains in factory work, and as manufacturing industries finally look to India, the numbers are beginning to add up. For instance, because Indian gem cutters earn 20 percent of what Europeans earn for the same work, much of the diamond-cutting and -polishing industry has migrated from Belgium to India, creating at least 500,000 jobs for Indians. With India's 140-million-strong mobile-phone market growing fast, Motorola and Nokia are building handset factories in India. The German auto parts maker Robert Bosch doubled its initially planned investment to $390 million. General Motors announced it would build a second car factory in India, betting that more and more Indians will soon be able to afford cars as more jobs are created. Some of the gains come when developed nations level the playing field: when the United States and Europe removed thirty-year-old textile quotas in 2005, Indian textile factories prospered. Exports to the United States alone jumped 36 percent, with Indians delivering textiles for The Gap, Crate & Barrel, and the like.

A Plan for Rural Workers

While Chinese development favors factory exports, perhaps the biggest potential source of growth in India comes from the countryside, where most Indians live. Sixty percent of India's workers and a third of its economic output are dependent on agriculture. Politicians dream of creating jobs in rural areas as a quick way to bring gains to India's poorest, and as a way to discourage mass migration into already teeming cities. The developed world is partly to blame for the fact that India does not export more from its farms. Western nations have balked at cutting subsidies for their farmers, which often price Indian exports out of the market. The European Union famously pays its farmers two dollars per cow in daily subsidies, more than most Indian *people* subsist on each day.

But India's lack of infrastructure is a big hurdle even to farmers. Not only do many villages do without the electricity and water pumps that could help irrigate fields, but they are also hamstrung by India's poor highway network after they

Agriculture Expert M.S. Swaminathan Analyzes India's Food Crisis

In India, farmers are growing crops for ethanol on their farm lands. This should be restricted to degraded land. I am opposed to prime land being used to grow fuel. . . .

Our soil is hungry and thirsty. It lacks a variety of nutrients, but our policies have favoured only nitrogen.

The other major issue is the need for the government to start soil-testing laboratories that can spread out to every district in the country and offer farmers a health card on their soil. The only state that has invested in this so far is Gujarat. We also need to focus on water and. . . .

Give importance to irrigation, especially in states like Jharkhand and Chhattisgarh which are all single-crop areas. But food production of millet, bajra and other drought-tolerant crop varieties must also be encouraged. We are presently importing pulses and oilseed at very high prices. That is why I feel farmers in drought areas need a lot of support.

M.S. Swaminathan, as told to Rashme Sehgal, Info Change News & Features, April 2008. www.infochangeindia.org.

manage to harvest crops. With little refrigeration available, 40 percent of India's fruits and vegetables spoil before reaching markets because getting them from farms to stores over India's dirt roads and potholed highways takes so long. One of India's leading businessmen, Mukesh Ambani, chairman of Reliance Industries, India's biggest company, plans to change all that. He is spending a remarkable $5 billion to change the way India's agricultural industry works—from the financing of seeds to where produce is sold.

First Mr. Ambani plans to build 1,600 farm-supply stores nationwide, which will sell seeds, fertilizer, and fuel and provide farmers with credit to buy them. When fields are harvested, farmers could sell their crops to the same stores. Mr. Ambani's plan is patterned after one pioneered in northern India by Tata Chemicals, the chemical and fertilizer arm of the Tata Group. Its Kisan Sansar ("farm center") network of one-stop farming stores caters to more than twenty thousand villages and four million farmers in three provinces, but outdated Indian regulations prevent Tata from expanding the network nationwide. These farming centers are revolutionary in India. Up until now, farmers had to pay usurious rates to borrow from local money-lenders who sometimes charge more than 10 percent per day. A bad monsoon season typically cripples the harvest and bankrupts farmers who cannot repay the costly loans, their debt rising to perhaps $1,000. In 2005, hundreds of farmers escaped their debt by killing themselves, often by drinking fertilizer. The existence of loans for farmers at fair prices would make the consequences of a failed harvest much less tragic. Mr. Ambani also plans to build eighty-five modern logistics hubs to move the produce from the farm-supply stores to customers, some in India and some overseas.

Perhaps the most ambitious part of his plan is to change the way the food is sold, bypassing India's remarkable number of mom-and-pop shops, which now sell 96 percent of India's goods. Mr. Ambani wants to build the Wal-Mart of India, creating a chain of stores across India to sell the produce and other goods. At the same time, a modern distribution system would get produce to ports and airports, creating $20 billion in agricultural exports, by Mr. Ambani's estimation....

India Must Seize the Moment

India is at a critical juncture. If the nation fails to create jobs for its fast-growing population of workers, it risks being mired in poverty and hopelessness. The Indian government is portraying the nation's population growth as a huge global advantage. For that to prove true, the government must not squander an opportunity to promote the economic growth that will provide jobs for all those new workers in coming decades. Because the offshoring phenomenon has attracted the attention of foreign companies, India is finally having its moment on the world economic stage. The Indian government must seize this historic chance. It must further reform its economy and modernize the nation's infrastructure, encouraging Indian companies to grow at the same time it attracts the foreign-built factories that will create jobs at home, much as China has done so successfully during the past decade.

"A unique constellation of factors now objectively indicate that India is now on the threshold of a golden age of growth," said the former finance secretary Vijay Kelkar. "If we seize this moment, India can transit out of poverty, and coming generations can enjoy an era of unprecedented prosperity and a decisive voice in shaping the global economic order and world politics." But he offered a warning too: "It is necessary that we choose wisely because wrong choices now can mean all future generations would remain poor forever."

So far, India's record is frustratingly mixed, and the challenge is primarily political. Foreign political commentators were stunned when the government of Prime Minister Atal Bihari Vajpayee was resoundingly defeated in 2004. They were surprised because India's economy was prospering its offshoring industry creating so many new jobs that Vajpayee's campaign slogan was "India Shining." The poor—the majority—revolted and voted him out of office. India was not shining for them. In fact, the poor were watching compatriots get ahead while their lives had changed little. Politicians and business leaders alike have come to a postelection consensus that India must find a way to give its poor better prospects. "Having two Indias will not work," said Mr. Nilekani of Infosys. "Because of the democratic system, any strategy will have to involve getting more equitable growth. Politically, you will have to carry everyone on that journey."

After Mr. Vajpayee's 2004 defeat, the next government was a coalition of various parties, led by the Congress Party. To appease the poor, one of the new government's earliest endeavors was the National Rural Employment Guarantee Act, passed in parliament in 2005, which guarantees a hundred days of work a year to every rural household that wants it at pay around the average minimum-wage level of $1.35 a day. Because of the sheer numbers of India's poor population, the cost is a staggering $9.1 billion, or 1.3 percent of India's GDP at a time when the government is already running a large deficit. The jobs program will function as a bare-bones safety net for the very poor, but the biggest economic lift would come from the creation of private-sector jobs. . . .

Encourage Investment in India

Without changes, job creation will stall, and the very poor—the ones politicians claim they are protecting—will continue to suffer. "We have to create this as an engine that pulls the whole economy. You need to create manufacturing jobs, service and farm jobs," said Mr. Nilekani. India's IT [information technology] industry "can't be the only game in town. It may only create jobs for a few million people. This is a terrific engine which is pulling the train, but we can't allow the engine to go ahead and let the rest of the train sit in the siding."

What China accomplishes by fiat, India must accomplish partly through persuasion. To move its economic development forward, India must come to grips with the nation's enduring postcolonial aversion to connecting to the world economy, and it must put in place policies that encourage Indian and foreign companies to hire in India. The Indian government must master the delicate politics of the poor. India has by far more poor people than those in the middle class; McKinsey calculates that 110 million Indian households—about 550 million people—make do on incomes between $1,500 and $4,000 a year, and an additional 40 million households are simply destitute, scraping by on less that $1,500 a year. They may be poor, but they are not quite powerless: in India, the poor vote in great numbers, and the middle class often skips the voting booth—almost the opposite of the pattern in the United States. The Indian government must convince voters that the changes it uses to spur economic development will bring them gains—something that is sometimes easier to see from a distance. It must make the case that building new roads will create hundreds of thousands of construction jobs for the poor even as it displaces some from their homes. It must argue that allowing foreign companies to build new factories will bring steady paychecks to hundreds of thousands more. It must argue that allowing new retail stores to compete with traditional mom-and-pop shops will result in both lower prices and more jobs created than lost. And if the government fails to carry those arguments—as it has so far—it must be content to let companies like Mr. Murthy's Infosys, Mr. Ambani's Reliance Industries, and Mr. Tata's Tata Group make the changes the government cannot. Unlike China, where the government spearheads change by championing big development projects, India may need to let private companies lead the way.

Periodical Bibliography

The following articles have been selected to supplement the diverse views presented in this chapter.

Md Mudassir Alam "India's Secular Character Under Threat," Merinews.com, August 28, 2008.

Jagdish Bhagwati "Secularism in India: Why Is It Imperiled?" December 2005. www.columbia.edu.

Nandan Desai "US India Nuclear Deal: When Economic Dreams Meet Geopolitical Reality," Indian Economy Blog, December 4, 2006. http://indianeconomy.org.

Subir Gokarn "What's the Solution to Global Food Crisis?" Rediff India Abroad, April 7, 2008.

IndiaKnowledge@ Wharton "In India, Will Corruption Slow Growth or Will Growth Slow Corruption?" University of Pennsylvania, August 8, 2007.

Afsar Jafri "Food Crisis Exposes Failings of India's Agricultural Reforms," *Mainstream*, August 2, 2008.

R.A. Jahagirdar "Secularism in India—The Inconclusive Debate," International Humanist and Ethical Union, May 11, 2003.

Daryl G. Kimball and Fred McGoldrick "U.S.-Indian Nuclear Agreement: A Bad Deal Gets Worse," Arms Control Association, August 3, 2007.

Press Trust of India "N-Deal Fully Consistent with India's Interests, says Centre," Rediff India Abroad, October 20, 2008.

Toronto Star "India Deserves Our Support on Nuke Deal," August 8, 2008.

Martin Walker "India's Path to Greatness," *Wilson Quarterly*, Summer 2006.

For Further Discussion

Chapter 1

1. Greenpeace India Society and Iain Murray arrive at different conclusions about whether India should be required to reduce its emissions. Explain how the authors use similar statistics to support opposing arguments. State why you think India should or should not be required to reduce its emissions.

2. Rabindra P. Kar and Daniel W. Drezner both discuss negative effects of outsourcing on India. Do you think accepting outsourced jobs benefits or hurts India? Cite facts from the viewpoints.

Chapter 2

1. Pankaj Mishra contends that India's treatment of Kashmir is radicalizing the people and driving them toward religious extremism. Examine the statements he makes in support of this claim and decide whether or not you agree with it. Explain.

2. In the viewpoint by Julia Duin, the author explains that some Indians believe it is better to abort a female fetus than to give a girl up for adoption. How do you think this mindset might affect the gender gap in India in the future?

Chapter 3

1. The organization Asha-Kiran contends that the dowry law is being misused by urban educated women and their families as 'an assassin's weapon'. How do you think Rakesh Shukla might respond to this claim? Support your answer.

2. R. Arun Kumar's viewpoint originally appeared in a publication of the Communist Party of India (Marxist). How do you think his political background could be affecting his argument that reservations are needed for equality?

3. M.R. Venkatesh directly addresses the reader at times. How does this style impact his argument, in your opinion? Is his style attention-getting, or distracting, for example? Explain.

4. Choose one of the myths of child labor as set forth by Bruce Stokes, and evaluate the author's response. Do you think it is well-reasoned and supported? Do you agree with him? Why or why not?

Chapter 4

1. What is Meera Nanda's tone toward educated men and women who are becoming more religious? What does the author imply when describing such people as believers in "supernatural powers supposedly embodied in idols?" Do you think this strengthens or weakens her argument? Cite the viewpoint in your answer.

Organizations to Contact

The editors have compiled the following list of organizations concerned with the issues debated in this book. The descriptions are derived from materials provided by the organizations. All have publications or information available for interested readers. The list was compiled on the date of publication of the present volume; the information provided here may change. Be aware that many organizations take several weeks or longer to respond to inquiries, so allow as much time as possible.

American India Foundation (AIF)
216 East Forty-Fifth Street, 7th Floor, New York, NY   10017
(646) 530-8977 • fax: (212) 661-9350
e-mail: info@aif.org
Web site: www.aifoundation.org

The nonprofit American India Foundation (AIF) works toward social and economic improvement in India. It has invested in over one hundred non-governmental organizations in India and has established service programs through which American professionals can volunteer and conduct research. AIF publishes press releases and a quarterly newsletter, and published the book *Locked Homes, Empty Schools*, about migrant worker families in India.

Amnesty International (AI)
C/O IMP, Peter Benenson House, 1 Easton Street
London   WC1X 0DW
    United Kingdom
e-mail: amnestyis@amnesty.org
Web site: www.amnesty.org

Amnesty International (AI) is a worldwide movement that campaigns for internationally recognized human rights. It has printed articles on India in its quarterly newsletter *Amnesty*

Action. Its Web site contains press releases, news stories, and reports such as *Amnesty International Report 2008: Republic of India.*

Brookings Institution
1775 Massachusetts Avenue NW, Washington, DC   20036
(202) 797-6000
Web site: www.brookings.org

Founded in 1927, the Brookings Institution conducts research and analyzes global events and their impact on the United States and U.S. foreign policy. The institution publishes the quarterly *Brookings Review,* as well as numerous books and research papers on foreign policy.

Center for Strategic and International Studies (CSIS)
1800 K Street NW, Suite 400, Washington, DC   26006
(202) 887-0200 • fax: (202) 775-3199
Web site: www.csis.org

Since its formation in 1962, the Center for Strategic and International Studies (CSIS) has provided world leaders with strategic insights and policy options on current and emerging global issues. CSIS disseminates a monthly newsletter, the *South Asian Monitor,* that covers events in the region, as well as the *Washington Quarterly* journal on political, economic, and security issues. Reports accessible on its Web site include *India as a Global Power?*

Center for the Advanced Study of India (CASI)
University of Pennsylvania, Philadelphia, PA   19104-3106
(215) 898-6247 • fax: (215) 573-2595
e-mail: casi@sas.upenn.edu
Web site: www.sas.upenn.edu/casi

Founded in 1992, the Center for the Advanced Study of India (CASI) is the only institute in the United States that focuses on the study of contemporary India. CASI sponsors research projects and distributes information on India's changing politics, society, and economy. Find reports, papers, and speeches on its Web site, as well as its online publication, *India in Transition.*

Embassy of India

2107 Massachusetts Avenue NW, Washington, DC   20008
(202) 939-7000 • fax: (202) 265-4351
e-mail: info2@indiagov.org
Web site: www.indianembassy.org

The embassy offers general information on India and provides consular services. Its Web site provides reference documents, policy statements, speeches by Indian government officials, and reprints of articles from Indian newspapers.

Freedom House

1319 Eighteenth Street NW, Washington, DC   20036
(202) 296-5101
Website: www.freedomhouse.org

Freedom House promotes human rights, democracy, free market economics, the rule of law, and independent media around the world. It publishes *Freedom in the World,* an annual comparative assessment of the state of political rights and civil liberties in one hundred and ninety-one countries.

National Portal of India

National Portal Secretariat, New Delhi   110 003
    India
e-mail: indiaportal@gov.in
Web site: http://india.gov.in

The National Portal of India is the country's official government site. It contains a wealth of country information, including statistics, news, maps, tourist advisories, and reports in English and Hindi. The Web site includes publications and guidelines pertaining to education, technology, rural development, water conservation, business, and other topics.

United States Department of State,
Bureau of South Asian Affairs
2201 C Street NW, Washington, DC   20520
(202) 647-4000
e-mail: secretary@state.gov
Web site: www. state.gov/p/eap

The United States Department of State, Bureau of South Asian Affairs deals with U.S. foreign relations and policy with the countries in South Asia. Information about India is available on its Web site along with news briefings and press statements on U.S. foreign policy. The archive and "Background Notes" on India provide useful facts.

Bibliography of Books

Sanjay K. Agarwal   *Corporate Social Responsibility in India*. New Delhi: Sage, 2008.

Robert D. Baird, ed.   *Religion and Law in Independent India*. New Delhi: Manohar, 2005.

Rashmi Dube Bhatnagar and Reena Dube   *Female Infanticide in India*. Albany, NY: State University of New York, 2005.

Center for Human Rights & Global Justice and Human Rights Watch   *Hidden Apartheid: Caste Discrimination Against India's "Untouchables."* New York: 2007.

Paul Davies   *What's This India Business?: Offshoring, Outsourcing, and the Global Services Revolution*. Boston: Nicholas Brealey, 2008.

Rafiq Dossani   *India Arriving: How This Economic Powerhouse Is Redefining Global Business*. New York: AMACOM, 2007.

Dipankar Gupta   *Caste in Question: Identity or Hierarchy*. New Delhi: Sage, 2004.

Zoya Hasan, E. Sridharan, and R. Sudarshan, eds.   *India's Living Constitution*. London: Anthem Press, 2005.

Geoff Hiscock   *India's Store Wars: Retail Revolution and the Battle for the Next 500 Million Shoppers*. Hoboken, NJ: Wiley, 2008.

Sarah Hodges, ed.   *Reproductive Health in India.* New Delhi: Orient Longman, 2006.

Gary Jeffrey Jacobsohn   *The Wheel of Law: India's Secularism in Comparative Constitutional Context.* Princeton, NJ: Princeton University, 2005.

Christophe Jaffrelot, ed.   *Hindu Nationalism: A Reader.* Princeton, NJ: Princeton University, 2007.

Mira Kamdar   *Planet India: The Turbulent Rise of the Largest Democracy and the Future of Our World.* New York: Scribner, 2008.

Yasmin Khan   *The Great Partition: The Making of India and Pakistan.* New Haven, CT: Yale University, 2007.

Ravi Kumar, ed.   *The Crisis of Elementary Education in India.* New Delhi: Sage, 2006.

K. Kusum   *Harassed Husbands.* New Delhi: Regency, 2003.

Edward Luce   *In Spite of the Gods: The Strange Rise of Modern India.* New York: Anchor, 2008.

John McGuire and Ian Copland, eds.   *Hindu Nationalism and Governance.* New Delhi: Oxford University Press, 2007.

Dinshaw Mistry   *Containing Missile Proliferation.* Seattle, WA: University of Washington, 2005.

Meera Nanda — *God and Globalization in India.* New Delhi: Navayana Publishers, forthcoming.

Anuradha Dingwaney Needham and Rajeswari Sunder Rajan, eds. — *The Crisis of Secularism in India.* Durham, NC: Duke University, 2006.

Martha C. Nussbaum — *The Clash Within: Democracy, Religious Violence, and India's Future.* Cambridge, MA: Harvard University, 2007.

Harsh V. Pant — *Contemporary Debates in Indian Foreign and Security Policy.* New York: Palgrave MacMillan, 2008.

T.V. Paul, ed. — *The India-Pakistan Conflict.* New York: Cambridge University, 2005.

Mohan Rao — *From Population Control to Reproductive Health.* New Delhi: Sage, 2005.

Narendra Singh Sarila — *The Shadow of the Great Game: The Untold Story of India's Partition.* New York: Carroll & Graf, 2006.

Mary Scaria — *Woman: An Endangered Species?* New Delhi: Media House, 2006.

Mala Sen — *Death by Fire: Sati, Dowry Death, and Female Infanticide in Modern India.* New Brunswick, NJ: Rutgers University, 2002.

Vandana Shiva   *India Divided: Diversity and Democracy Under Attack*. New York: Seven Stories, 2005.

Mrinalini Sinha   *Specters of Mother India: The Global Restructuring of an Empire*. Durham, NC: Duke University, 2006.

Shashi Tharoor   *The Elephant, the Tiger, and the Cell Phone*. New York: Arcade, 2008.

Sukhadeo Thorat and Narender Kumar, eds.   *In Search of Inclusive Policy; Addressing Graded Inequality*. New Delhi: Rawat, 2008.

Ashutosh Varshney   *Ethnic Conflict and Civic Life: Hindus and Muslims in India*. New Haven, CT: Yale University, 2003.

Vivek   *Lies, Lies, and More Lies: The Campaign to Defame Hindu/Indian Nationalism*. Bloomington, IN: iUniverse, 2007.

Myron Weiner, Neera Burra, and Asha Bajpai   *Born Unfree: Child Labour, Education, and the State in India*. New Delhi: Oxford University, 2006.

Index